READ WELL®

Getting Started

A Guide to Implementation
Units 1-26 and Review Units

Sopris West™
EDUCATIONAL SERVICES

A Cambium Learning Company

BOSTON, MA • LONGMONT, CO

**Critical Foundations
in Primary Reading**

**Marilyn Sprick • Shelley V. Jones
Richard Dunn • Barbara Gunn**

13 12 11 10 09 08   3 4 5 6

ISBN 13-digit: 978-1-59318-740-8
ISBN 10-digit: 1-59318-740-8

Printed in the United States of America
Published and Distributed by

Sopris West™
EDUCATIONAL SERVICES

A Cambium Learning Company

4093 Specialty Place • Longmont, CO 80504 • 303-651-2829
www.sopriswest.com

Photo Credits: Cover, Title page: ©Rubber Ball

Illustration Credits: Ants, ABC Wall Card illustrations, and Theo Bear by Philip E. Weber. Jr., Mr. E. Men, and Tom Zilis. ii-iii: House and rabbits by Larry Nolte. iv: Cat by Tom Zilis, Landscape by Anna Ochoa. vi: Tiger by Kevin McDonnell. 66: CHICKA CHICKA BOOM BOOM cover courtesy of Aladdin/Simon & Schuster. LOBSTER'S SECRET image courtesy of Soundprints, an imprint of Trudy Corporation, Norwalk, CT. THE LISTENING WALK cover courtesy of HarperCollins Children's Books. GENTLE GIANT OCTOPUS cover. Text copyright © 1998 Karen Wallace. Illustrations copyright © 1998 Mike Bostock. Reproduced by permission of the publisher, Candlewick Press, Inc., Cambridge, MA, on behalf of Walker Books Ltd., London. THE BABY BEEBEE BIRD cover courtesy of HarperCollins Children's Books. 74: Cat by Tom Zilis. 101: Cover by Eric Carle from BROWN BEAR, BROWN BEAR, WHAT DO YOU SEE? Text by Bill Martin, Jr., Illustration © 1992 by Eric Carle. Reprinted by permission of Henry Holt and Company, LLC. THE LISTENING WALK cover courtesy of HarperCollins Children's Books. GREEN EGGS AND HAM cover courtesy of Random House. CAPS FOR SALE cover courtesy of HarperCollins Children's Books. FRIENDS cover courtesy of Aladdin/Simon & Schuster. THE BABY BEEBEE BIRD cover courtesy of HarperCollins Children's Books. THE COW THAT WENT OINK cover used with permission of Harcourt, Inc. Cover of TWO BAD ANTS by Chris Van Allsburg. Copyright © 1988 by Chris Van Allsburg. Reprinted by permission of Houghton Mifflin Company. All rights reserved. THE BERENSTAIN BEARS AND TOO MUCH JUNK FOOD cover courtesy of Random House. Cover from MADELINE by Ludwig Bemelmans, copyright 1939 by Ludwig Bemelmans, renewed © 1967 by Madeline Bemelmans and Barbara Bemelmans Marciano. Used by permission of Viking Penguin, A Division of Penguin Young Readers Group (USA) Inc., 345 Hudson Street, New York, NY 10014. All rights reserved. Cover from OFFICER BUCKLE AND GLORIA by Peggy Rathman, copyright © 1995 by Peggy Rathman. Used by permission of G. P. Putnam's Sons, A Division of Penguin Young Readers group, A Member of Penguin Group (USA) Inc., 345 Hudson Street, New York, NY 10014. All rights reserved. From HONK!: THE STORY OF A PRIMA SWANERINA by Pamela Duncan Edwards. Copyright © 1999. Cover reprinted by permission of Hyperion Books for Children. All rights reserved. Jacket design from MOSES GOES TO A CONCERT by Isaac Millman. Copyright (c) 1998 by Isaac Millman. Reprinted by permission of Farrar, Straus and Giroux, LLC. MISS TIZZY cover courtesy of Aladdin/Simon & Schuster. HONEY: A GIFT FROM NATURE cover courtesy of Kane/Miller Book Publishers. THE CARROT SEED cover courtesy of HarperCollins Children's Books. JUST YOU AND ME cover. Text copyright © 1998 Sam McBratney. Illustration copyright © 1998 Ivan Bates. Reproduced by permission of the publisher, Candlewick Press, Inc., Cambridge, MA, on behalf of Walker Books Ltd., London. LOBSTER'S SECRET image courtesy of Soundprints, an imprint of Trudy Corporation, Norwalk, CT. GENTLE GIANT OCTOPUS. Text copyright © 1998 Karen Wallace. Illustrations copyright © 1998 Mike Bostock. Reproduced by permission of the publisher, Candlewick Press, Inc., Cambridge, MA, on behalf of Walker Books Ltd., London. Cover from MAMA DO YOU LOVE ME?: text © 1991 by Barbara M. Joosse; illustrations © 1991 by Barbara Lavallee. Used with permission of Chronicle Books LLC, San Francisco. Visit ChronicleBooks.com. THE RELATIVES CAME cover courtesy of Aladdin/Simon & Schuster. DR. SEUSS'S ABC cover courtesy of Random House.

Dear Teachers:

We are excited to bring you the second edition of *Read Well K*. In the years since the original *Read Well K* was published, we have continued to be inspired by teachers who with dedication and joy are helping thousands of children exceed expectations. We have been awed and humbled by the accomplishments and self-confidence of the young children we serve.

As parents, consultants, teachers, and consumers of research, we continue to be deeply committed to young children. We share your passion for preparing them for a successful and confident journey through school. We have a deep belief in what research has now validated—that what we do makes a difference.

Our Guiding Principles

- Children need to read well to feel like they belong in the world of school and in their communities.
- Despite differences in backgrounds and abilities, every child deserves to receive instruction that meets his or her individual needs.
- Early literacy instruction must be age and individually appropriate.
- Teaching young children to read well requires four things: (a) carefully designed instructional tools, (b) dedicated and skillful teachers who teach with enthusiasm, (c) sufficient amounts of instructional time, and (d) professional collaboration.

There are deep rewards in giving children a firm foundation in reading. Have Fun!

Sincerely,

Marilyn Sprick

Shelley V. Jones

Richard Dunn

Barbara Gunn

Dedicated to:

- Doug Carnine, who helped us understand how curriculum can be built to accommodate the needs of children

- Zig Engelmann, whose passion and brilliance taught us that excellence in instructional design can make a difference

- The school team of Carol Kirwan (kindergarten teacher), Mo Anderson (reading specialist), and Jo Robinson (principal) who demonstrated to us what *Read Well* could accomplish when combined with excellence in teaching, collaboration, and instructional leadership

Acknowledgements:

- Randy Sprick, author of the *Safe & Civil Schools* series, who shared his insights and knowledge as we addressed the important management considerations of young children

- The staffs at Teaching Strategies and Sopris West who monitored the important details as manuscripts were prepared and brought into final form

- The illustrators and designers who shared their talents in making this newest version of *Read Well K* a visual delight

- Story writers Jessica Sprick and LJ Sellers, who shared their talents and imagination

- Jon Melendy, who engineered and helped create the *Read Well K* CD of Songs

- The teachers who field tested *Read Well K*

- The many dedicated teachers who have given us ongoing feedback about the needs of children since the first publication of *Read Well K*

Read Well K Authors Who Teach!

Marilyn Sprick, M.S., is the senior author of the *Read Well* series. With degrees in psychology, education, and special education, Marilyn has worked as a general education teacher, Title I learning specialist, and special education teacher. As a consultant, Marilyn has worked with thousands of teachers across the country—adapting curriculum and instruction to better meet the needs of all students. The *Read Well* projects have allowed Marilyn to bring together her joy of teaching, her knowledge of research, and her enjoyment of artistic endeavors. From Eugene, Oregon, Marilyn and Randy Sprick co-direct Teaching Strategies, Inc.—a nationally recognized group of consultants who work with schools to improve student responsibility and academic success.

Shelley V. Jones, M. Mus., is a career educator and musician who has taught in Title 1, high-risk elementary schools as a music specialist, reading specialist, and kindergarten teacher. In her capacity as a reading specialist and *Read Well* trainer, Shelley has supervised and consulted with countless appreciative teachers and instructional assistants. As a music specialist, Shelley has been recognized for her eclectic and innovative music curriculum development, her song compositions, and her musical productions. Shelley has combined her love of music and reading in co-authoring and field-testing the *Read Well K* materials. In addition to helping create *Read Well K* as a whole, the *Read Well* CD of Songs is the result of Shelley's considerable talents.

Richard Dunn, B.S., is a practicing kindergarten teacher and *Read Well* trainer. As a first grade teacher, Richard was part of the original *Read Well 1* field test group. Richard's zeal for *Read Well*, in combination with endless energy and creativity, resulted in the creation of multiple thematic connections for his first graders. Richard's appreciation of kindergarten children is reflected in all aspects of *Read Well K*. Prior to teaching, Richard worked with developmentally disabled adults. Richard's background in psychology brought a unique perspective to the development of the program.

Barbara Gunn, Ph.D., is a reasearcher at Oregon Research Institute, studying early childhood literacy development and instructional approaches for developing beginning reading skills among Spanish- and English-speaking students. Barbara is an experienced elementary general education teacher. She completed her doctoral studies in special education at the University of Oregon and has published book chapters and journal articles that focus on the development of emergent literacy and beginning reading instruction. Barbara brought her research-based knowledge to the development of *Read Well* and found, in the process, a talent for writing stories.

Table of Contents

Section 1 — Program Overview

Section 2 — Getting the Year Started

Who Is
Read Well K For?

Read Well K's developmental framework meets the needs of all kindergarten children—from those with intensive instructional needs to those with advanced reading skills.

Kindergarten Students

Read Well K is for general education kindergarten students, both prereaders and beginning readers.

Read Well K has two components.

Read Well K Whole Class helps children get ready for reading.

Age Appropriate: Whole Class provides young children with age appropriate instruction in oral language, phonemic awareness, phonics, vocabulary, and comprehension skills. Whole Class instruction is paced for the enjoyment of all.

Read Well K Small Group gets children reading.

Individually Appropriate: Small Group provides young children with individually appropriate instruction in oral language, phonemic awareness, phonics, fluency, vocabulary, and comprehension skills. Small Group instruction is paced for individual mastery of critical skills.

Primary Grade Students With Special Needs

Special Education Students in Self-Contained Classrooms: *Read Well K* Whole Class may be used with special populations in full-day programs.

Intervention: *Read Well K* Small Group is an effective intervention, especially when used in combination with *Read Well 1* and *Read Well 1 Spelling and Writing Conventions*.

Program Overview

In this section:

Features of *Read Well K*

Research Based

> **Oral Language**
> **Phonemic Awareness**
> **Phonics**
> **Vocabulary**
> **Comprehension**
> **Fluency**

Just Right for Young Children
Research findings provided the road map for the development of *Read Well K,* which includes each area of instructional focus recommended through scientific research studies.

Teacher-Friendly
The authors, who are experienced teachers, created rich and teacher-friendly applications.

Developmentally Appropriate

Read Well K is developmentally appropriate with practices that are both age and individually appropriate. *Read Well K* Whole Class is age appropriate, and *Read Well K* Small Group is individually appropriate.

Learning to read and write is one of the most important and powerful achievements in life. Its value is clearly seen in the faces of young children— the proud, confident smile of the capable reader contrasts sharply with the furrowed brow and sullen frown of the discouraged nonreader. Ensuring that all young children reach their potentials as readers and writers is the shared responsibility of teachers, administrators, families, and communities.

—Joint position of the International Reading Association (IRA) and National Association for the Education of Young Children (NAEYC), 1998

Age Appropriate

Young children benefit from interactions with children of diverse abilities, interests, and backgrounds. *Read Well K* Whole Class activities build a foundation of skills through carefully selected themes and activities.

Kinder-Friendly Themes . . .

Welcome children to school and the world around them.
Take a school tour.
Meet important people.
Go on a listening walk.

Build relationships.
Share with friends.
Play together.
Cheer each other on.

Captivate interest.
Study things that creep and crawl.

Teach important lessons of early childhood.
Learn how to eat well, stay well, and be safe.

Honor home and family.
Celebrate family traditions.

Features and Activities
- **Read Alouds**
- **Songs and Cheers**
- **Art Projects**
- **Games**
- **Pocket Chart**
- **Bookmaking**
- **Journals and White Boards**

Small Group

Individually Appropriate

Young children need to feel comfortable and competent as they develop the skills that allow them to become "ready to read." *Read Well K* Small Group instruction allows children to become readers at a pace that is appropriate to their development. Critical reading foundations are established during Small Group instruction. Regular individual assessment ensures that group placement and instruction are tailored to each child's needs.

Kinder-Friendly Themes . . .

Teach important lessons of early childhood.

Friends cheer each other on. Be a good sport.

Captivate interest.

Cats can talk with their tails.
A blue whale can be as large as three school buses!

Appreciate cultural diversity.

Look for a precious conch shell with a Hawaiian family.
Take a dogsled ride with an Inuit boy and his grandfather in the Arctic twilight.

Explore interesting jobs.

Get to know firefighters, paramedics, and cowgirls.

Share traditional tales and rhymes.

Hey Diddle, Diddle—why did the cow jump over the moon?

Features and Activities

- **Daily Mastery-Based Lessons**
- **Sound Practice**
- **Stretch and Shrink**
- **Sound Counting**
- **Smooth and Bumpy Blending**
- **Pattern Word Practice**
- **Daily Story Reading**
- **Ongoing Progress Monitoring**

What *Read Well K* Kids Can Do

High Success, Happy Children

Closing the Achievement Gap: Montgomery, Alabama

Before implementing *Read Well,* Montgomery scored **119th*** out of 130 districts in Alabama in grades K–2. At the end of the school year, after just one year with *Read Well,* Montgomery scored **17th*** in the state.† Montgomery students continue to show success, as illustrated below.

Kindergarten

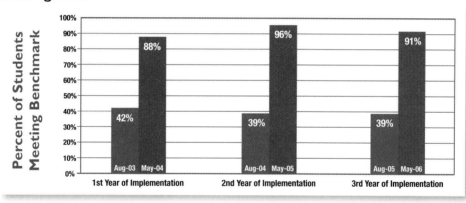

Lasting Effects

Research has shown that a child who is a poor reader at the end of first grade will remain a poor reader at the end of fourth grade 88% of the time.‡ *Read Well* students build a strong foundation of skills to ensure future reading success.

First Grade

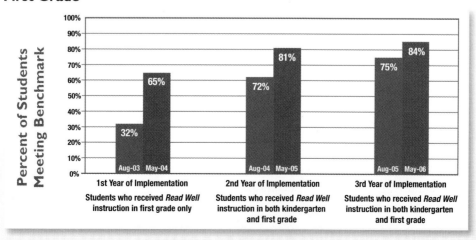

* as measured by (DIBELS) Dynamic Indicators of Basic Early Literacy Skills
† Source: Teresa Nichols, Ph.D., Retired Educational Specialist/Coordinator K–3 Reading, Montgomery Public Schools
‡ Source: Juel, 1988

What Can Your Children Achieve?

Data collected from schools that have implemented *Read Well* with fidelity have demonstrated that students who have had *Read Well K* in kindergarten and *Read Well 1* in first grade exceed expectations.

HIGH-PERFORMING STUDENTS

High-performing students in normal and high-risk populations who begin kindergarten knowing their sounds and a few sight words typically complete *Read Well K* before the end of their kindergarten year. These students proceed into *Read Well 1* during kindergarten, often finishing *Read Well 1* Unit 30. In first grade, these students finish *Read Well 1* and then proceed at a comfortable but accelerated pace in *Read Well Plus*. (First grade students who have completed *Read Well Plus* have scored between 2.8 and 4.9 grade equivalence on the Woodcock Reading Mastery Passage Comprehension Subtest.)

AVERAGE-PERFORMING STUDENTS

Average-performing students in normal and high-risk populations are accelerated, often achieving above-grade-level expectations by the end of first grade. By the end of their kindergarten year, most average-performing students are able to read *Read Well K* Units 12–15.

LOW-PERFORMING STUDENTS

By the end of their kindergarten year, most low-performing students are able to read *Read Well K* Unit 5. These same students are typically able to read *Read Well 1* Unit 30 by the end of first grade. This means students are about eight weeks shy of reaching grade level expectations. Students who would normally remain below grade level are then often able to achieve grade level expectations during their second grade year of school.

Read Well K Unit 20
Solo Story 4

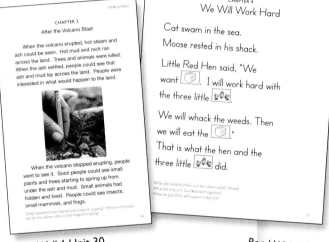

STORY 4, SOLO

CHAPTER 4
We Will Work Hard

Cat swam in the sea.
Moose rested in his shack.

Little Red Hen said, "We want ⬡. I will work hard with the three little 🐥🐥."

We will whack the weeds. Then we will eat the ⬡."

That is what the hen and the three little 🐥🐥 did.

Read Well 1 Unit 30
Solo Story 6

CHAPTER 2
After the Volcano Blast

When the volcano erupted, hot steam and ash could be seen. Hot mud and rock ran across the land. Trees and animals were killed. When the ash settled, people could see that ash and mud lay across the land. People were interested in what would happen to the land.

When the volcano stopped erupting, people went to see it. Soon people could see small plants and trees starting to spring up from under the ash and mud. Small animals had hidden and lived. People could see insects, small mammals, and frogs.

Read Well K Unit 12
Solo Story 4

STORY 4, SOLO

CHAPTER 2

The cat said, "See me. I'm 🐱."
The cat said, "I'm 🐱.
🐱 me. 🐱 me."
"We can see the sweet cat," said 🐸.
"We can 🐸 that cat."

CHAPTER 2
Sad Sam

Sam said, "See 1 🐷.
See 1 🕷.
See me."
"I'm sad," said Sam.

Read Well K Unit 5
Solo Story 4

Scientifically Based Reading Research

Why *Read Well* Works

All reading is based on a foundation of oral language. While oral language is developed naturally, reading is a learned skill—a complex mental activity that requires a sophisticated interaction between language, thought, and print.

The graphic organizer below reflects the objectives and strategies incorporated in *Read Well*. From and through oral language, *Read Well* provides explicit and systematic instruction in the five areas of instructional focus identified by researchers as being critical to reading with understanding. On a daily basis, students receive instruction in phonemic awareness, phonics, comprehension strategies, vocabulary, and fluency.*

The next pages provide snapshots of how *Read Well K* Whole Class and Small Group address each area of instructional focus.

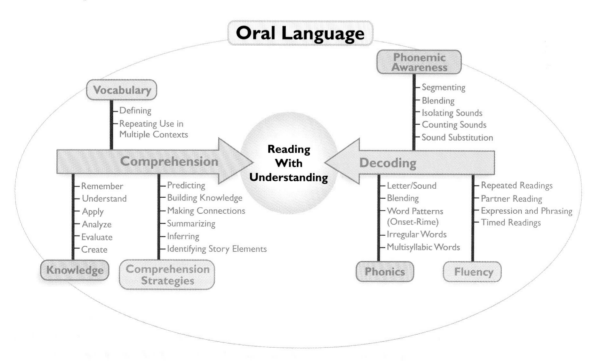

Graphic organizer adapted from Archer, 2000.

* Adams, 1990; Anderson, Hiebert, Scott, & Wilkinson, 1985; Armbruster, Lehr, & Osborn, 2001; National Reading Panel, 2000; Rayner, Foorman, Perfetti, Pesetsky, & Seidenberg, 2001; Torgesen, 2004. See the reference list on page 119.

Whole Class and Small Group Oral Language Priming

Research Snapshot

Independent Review of *Read Well*

"Read Well was found to have potentially positive effects on reading achievement of elementary school English language learners." (What Works Clearinghouse, U.S. Department of Education, Institute of Education Sciences, 2006).*

Read Well Is ELL Friendly

Read Well K is ELL friendly—with hundreds of Tips to help facilitate the development of English oral language. For children just learning English, *Read Well K* is the perfect complement to a structured English oral language program.

Read Well programming provides oral language priming of high-frequency words that will be read later by students. Before reading the words, students use the words repeatedly in natural oral language contexts. The next three pages outline an instructional sequence that moves students from using a word in spoken language, in both Whole Class and Small Group, to later reading the word in text.

USING WORDS IN CONVERSATION

ORAL LANGUAGE PRIMING OF . . . see

Following is a sample script from Whole Class Unit 2. It demonstrates how students use the word "see" as they observe the world around them through Art Project binoculars.

Pass out binoculars and practice.

We're going to take our binoculars with us.

When we stop, you can look through your binoculars.

I'll say "Class, class, what do you see?"

Then, I'll call on one of you to tell me what you see.

Let's try it.

Class, class, what do you see?

[Hector], you have your hand up.

◆◆What do you see? ([students])

Everyone, do you see [students]? (yes)

[Hector], say "I see [students]." (I see [students].)

ELL STUDENTS

Repeated practice in multiple contexts provides ELL students an opportunity to build their English oral language skills. Watch for the ◆◆ indicating oral language practice in activities such as Stretch and Shrink and Smooth and Bumpy Blending.

*Note: For research on Read Well with ELL students go to: http://www.whatworks.ed.gov/PDF/Intervention/WWC_Read_Well_092106.pdf

USING WORDS IN PHONEMIC AWARENESS ACTIVITIES

ORAL LANGUAGE PRIMING OF . . . see WITH STRETCH AND SHRINK

Following is a sample script from Small Group Unit 1. It demonstrates how to stretch and shrink the word "see" and then use it in a language pattern.

- Demonstrate orally stretching and shrinking "see." Then use "see" in an oral language pattern.
  Listen to me stretch and shrink the word see.
  Move your hands apart while stretching the word. /sssēēē/
  Move your hands together. see
  Who do you see? (I see [you].)

- Guide stretching the word.
  Now you try stretching the word see with me.
  Move your hands apart while stretching the word. /sssēēē/

- Guide shrinking the word.
  Shrink it up with me.
  Move your hands together. see

- Use the word in an oral language pattern.
  Who do you see? (I see [you].)

- Repeat, mixing group and individual turns, independent of your voice.

USING WORDS IN PHONICS ACTIVITIES

ORAL LANGUAGE PRIMING OF . . . see WITH SMOOTH AND BUMPY BLENDING

Smooth and Bumpy Blending exercises help children learn the difference between blending sounds smoothly and stopping or pausing between each sound. Smooth Blending paves the way to early and easy success in sounding out words. The Blending Cards show Hector Ant bumping along in a truck with a flat tire versus riding smoothly in a glider.

Whole Class and Small Group Oral Language Priming (continued)

READING OF . . . *see* IN WRITTEN CONTEXTS

Once students have practiced words in oral sentences, phonemic awareness activities, and blending practice, they read the words multiple times in multiple contexts during Whole Class instruction.

Whole Class Unit 15
Letter Book

Whole Class Unit 20
Sentence Scramble

READING WORDS IN CONTEXT

These pages demonstrate how words and language patterns are also embedded in Small Group Story Reading.

Read Well's unique duet format allows children to practice reading fully decodable text within meaningful sentences and stories. At Unit 4, students read words restricted to the letter/sound associations they have mastered with blending (s, e-e, e, m, a) and the word "I."

Small Group Unit 4, Story 5 Duet

Small Group Unit 4, Story 4 Solo

Small Group Unit 4, Story 3 Duet

Whole Class and Small Group
Alphabetic Knowledge and Phonological Awareness

ALPHABET ROUTINES

Whole Class takes children through the alphabet three times. In each unit, one new letter/sound association is introduced. Once a letter is introduced, review is continual from unit to unit.

To build letter-naming fluency, students regularly recite and sing the ABCs with *Boogie Woogie ABCs* and *Alphabet Beat*.

ORAL RHYMING

Whole Class activities frequently include oral rhyming in kinder-friendly activities. Students learn about rhyming with the master of rhyme, Dr. Seuss. Then explicit instruction is provided within the context of a Read Aloud from *Read Well's* Lap Book collection. From there, students play games and make art projects and puzzles with rhyming pairs.

RHYMING PATTERNS

Whole Class oral rhyming activities prepare students to recognize the visual patterns that correspond to the oral onsets and rimes. In Small Group, students sound out words and then learn to build accuracy and fluency with common letter patterns. After students read "at," "mat," "that," and "hat," they explain "the words are the same because they all end with -*at*."

Whole Class Unit 4, Lap Book 2

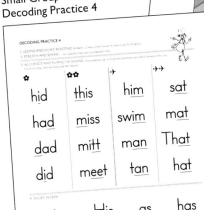

Small Group Unit 11 Magazine, Decoding Practice 4

Words that rhyme are lots of fun!
Mouse and house both end with … ouse.

This is the … mouse
who lives in a … house.

Whole Class Unit 5, Rhyming Game,
Mouse, Mouse, House

Whole Class Unit 6, Jigsaw Puzzle, Rhyming Picture Match

Whole Class Phonemic Awareness

Research Snapshot

Phonemic Awareness

Phonemic awareness is "the ability to notice, think about, and work with the individual sounds in spoken words" (Armbruster, Lehr, & Osborn, 2001).

Phonemic awareness has been found to both facilitate learning to read and to be a by-product of learning to read (Ehri et al., 2001).

Whole Class includes activities that both implicitly and explicitly teach young children about the sounds in speech.

Whole Class Unit 11, Poem Poster

UNIT 11

Quick Letter   D

Capital letter D,
Small letter d,
D says d.
11 dogs on a doghouse,
D, d, d.

HEARING SOUNDS IN WORDS • ALPHABET POEMS

Each day students recite poems that introduce and maintain letter/sound associations. In the last two lines of the poem, students practice the phonological skills of alliteration and isolating the beginning sound.

HEARING SOUNDS IN WORDS • ALPHABET CHEER

Daily recitation with the *Alphabet Cheer* provides fluency with the phonological skill of alliteration and the phonemic awareness skill of hearing and isolating beginning sounds.

The Cheer

A says /ăăă/. Ant on an apple, /ă/, /ă/, /ăăă/.
B, C, D.
E says /ēēē/. Eel on wheels, /ē/, /ē/, /ēēē/.
E . . .

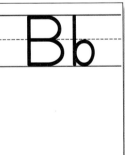

Aa	Bb	Cc	Dd	Ee
A says /ăăă/. Ant on an apple, /ă/, /ă/, /ăăă/.	B	C	D	E says /ēēē/. Eel on wheels, /ē/, /ē/, /ēēē/.

The ABC Wall Cards are two-sided and are turned over to show the corresponding image as each sound is introduced. (See page 61.) The new *Read Well K* CD of Songs includes a lively and whimsical sound track to support practice.

Research Snapshot

Blending and Segmenting

The National Reading Panel (2000) found that "teaching two PA [Phonemic Awareness] skills to children has a greater long-term benefit for reading than teaching only one PA skill or teaching a global array of skills." The two skills recommended for instruction are blending and segmenting. "Blending phonemes helps children to decode unfamiliar words. Segmenting words into phonemes helps children to spell unfamiliar words and also to retain spellings in memory" (Sec. 2, p. 21).

ORAL BLENDING

Stretch and Shrink is a quick part of the daily lesson in the Small Group units. Teachers tailor the amount of practice to students' needs. This script shows how to demonstrate oral blending of the word "am"—first introduced in Unit 4.

> The word is *am*. I *am* [Mrs. B].
> Listen to me stretch the word
> *am*. /ăăămmm/
> Now I'm going to shrink it up. am

Note: Words presented in Stretch and Shrink are later read in written text.

ORAL SEGMENTING

/ăăă/•/mmm/

In Preludes A–C and Units 1–3, students segment and count sounds. Sound counting is continued only with groups that require additional phonemic awareness instruction. (Segmenting continues on a daily basis in *Read Well Spelling and Writing Conventions*.)

Whole Class Phonics

Research Snapshot

Kindergarten Programs and Systematic Phonics

After a rigorous scientific review of multiple studies, the National Reading Panel (2000) concluded, " . . . results indicate clearly that systematic phonics instruction in kindergarten and 1st grade is highly beneficial and that children at these developmental levels are quite capable of learning phonemic and phonics concepts" (National Reading Panel, 2000, sec. 2–85).

Read Well K Whole Class Sequence of Sounds and Themes

Unit	Sound Sequence	Letter/Sound Associations	Themes and Kinder Lessons	Read Aloud Titles and Genres
1	Aa	/ăăă/ as in ant on an apple	*Hello* People in your school are there to help.	*Chicka Chicka Boom Boom,* Fiction • Rhyming Narrative *What a Wonderful, Wonderful Class,* Fiction • Narrative
2	Ee	/ēēē/ as in eel on wheels	*What Do You See?* See wonderful things when you stop and look.	*Brown Bear, Brown Bear, What Do You See?,* Fiction • Repetitive Narrative; *Mrs. B's Guessing Games,* Fiction • Narrative
3	Hh	/h/ as in horse in a house	*What Do You Hear?* Hear wonderful things when you stop and listen.	*The Listening Walk,* Fiction • Narrative *The Field Trip,* Fiction • Rhyming Narrative
4	Kk	/k/ as in kid in a kayak	*Rhyming Fun* Rhyming words are great fun.	*Green Eggs and Ham,* Fiction • Rhyming Narrative *Words That Rhyme,* Fiction • Rhyming Narrative *May We Kayak in Your School?,* Fiction • Rhyming Narrative
5	Mm	/mmm/ as in monkey on a mountain	*Monkey Business* It's important to be polite.	*Caps for Sale,* Fiction • Narrative *Straw Hats for Sale,* Fiction • Narrative
6	Rr	/rrr/ as in rooster on the roof	*Make New Friends and Keep the Old* Good friends always stick together.	*Friends,* Fiction • Narrative *With a Little Help From Your Friends,* Fiction • Narrative *Friendship,* Nonfiction • Realistic
7	Ss	/sss/ as in spider in the soup	*Spiders Spinning* Spiders are interesting animals.	*The Very Busy Spider,* Fiction • Narrative *Spider Facts,* Nonfiction • Expository *Sahale, Master Weaver,* Fiction • Narrative
8	Ww	/www/ as in worm in a wagon	*Worms Crawling* Worms are more useful than you think.	*Wonderful Worms,* Nonfiction • Expository *Earthworm Facts,* Nonfiction • Expository *Alice's Adventures in Wormland,* Fiction • Narrative
9	Zz	/zzz/ as in zebra in the zoo	*What's Happening at the Zoo?* Everyone has a special way of seeing things.	*The Baby Beebee Bird,* Fiction • Narrative *Short Sam,* Fiction • Realistic Narrative
Rev (1–9)	Aa, Ee, Hh, Kk, Mm, Rr, Ss, Ww, Zz	/ăăă/, /ēēē/, /h/, /k/, /mmm/, /rrr/, /sss/, /www/, /zzz/	*Review* Practice makes perfect.	*(Review of children's favorite stories)*
10	Cc	/k/ as in cow on a cab	*Home, Home on the Farm* Never give up. Keep on trying.	*The Cow That Went OINK,* Fiction • Narrative *Old MacDonald's Farm,* Fiction • Narrative
11	Dd	/d/ as in dog on a doghouse	*Home Sweet Home* Dogs and people can help each other.	*The Adventures of Taxi Dog,* Fiction • Narrative *Sarge the Police Dog,* Fiction • Narrative With Factual Content *Helping Dogs,* Nonfiction • Expository
12	Ii	/ĭĭĭ/ as in insect in the ink	*Home Again, Home Again* There is no place like home.	*Two Bad Ants,* Fiction • Narrative *Insect Facts,* Nonfiction • Expository *Mrs. B's Anatomy Lesson,* Fiction • Narrative With Factual Content
13	Jj	/j/ as in jellybean in the jar	*Eating Well* Eat healthy foods to stay well.	*The Berenstain Bears and Too Much Junk Food,* Fiction • Narrative; *The Jellybean Junk Food Blues,* Fiction • Narrative *The Jefferson Park Blues,* Fiction • Narrative
14	Nn	/nnn/ as in nurse in the night	*Staying Well* People will help you if you have an accident.	*Madeline,* Fiction • Realistic Narrative *Look Where You're Going,* Fiction • Realistic Narrative
15	Pp	/p/ as in policeman in the park	*Keeping Safe* Call 9-1-1 in an emergency.	*Officer Buckle and Gloria,* Fiction • Narrative *Jonathan,* Poem *Call 9-1-1,* Fiction • Realistic Narrative

(continued)

Research Snapshot

Phonics and Content

"From the earliest ages, reading is much more than decoding . . . If we want to raise later achievement and avoid the fourth-grade slump, we need to combine early instruction in the procedures of literacy with early instruction in the content of literacy, specifically: vocabulary, conventions of language, and knowledge of the world" (Chall & Jacobs, 2003, p. 21).

Unit	Sound Sequence	Letter/Sound Associations	Themes and Kinder Lessons	Read Aloud Titles and Genres
16	Tt	/t/ as in turtle on a tightrope	*The Show Must Go On* Keep on trying.	***Honk!,*** Fiction • Narrative ***Tito Sings,*** Fiction • Narrative
17	Vv	/vvv/ as in violin in the van	*Music To My Ears* You can be anything when you grow up.	***Moses Goes to a Concert,*** Fiction • Narrative ***Just Right for You, Verdi Mouse,*** Fiction • Narrative
18	Yy	/y-/ as in yak in the yard	*Time For A Play* Performing can be joyful.	***Miss Tizzy,*** Fiction • Narrative ***The Case of the Missing Scarf,*** Fiction • Mystery
Short Vowel E and Rev	Ĕĕ	/ĕĕĕ/ as in Ed in the engine	*Review* Favorite stories are fun to read again.	*(Review of children's favorite stories)*
19	Bb	/b/ as in bee at the beach	*Bees Buzzing* Bees can do great things.	***Honey: A Gift From Nature,*** Fiction • Narrative With Factual Content; ***Bee Facts,*** Nonfiction • Expository ***Billy Bee Out West,*** Fiction • Narrative
20	Ff	/fff/ as in flower in the field	*Flowers Growing* Good things happen when you share.	***The Carrot Seed,*** Fiction • Narrative ***Flower Facts,*** Nonfiction • Expository ***Felicia's Flower,*** Fiction • Narrative
21	Gg	/g/ as in goose in the grass	*Mother Goose* Parents always love their children.	***Just You and Me,*** Fiction • Narrative ***Meet Mother Goose,*** Poems • Nursery Rhymes ***Goose, Goose, Goose, Goose, Duck,*** Fiction • Narrative
22	Ll	/lll/ as in lobster in the lighthouse	*Lobster's Lesson* Be kind to others.	***Lobster's Secret,*** Fiction • Narrative With Factual Content ***The Lobster Café,*** Fiction • Narrative
23	Oo	/ŏŏŏ/ as in octopus in the office	*Octopus Tales* Octopuses are intelligent.	***Gentle Giant Octopus,*** Nonfiction • Narrative ***From the Library of the Jellyfish Hotel,*** Fiction • Narrative ***How Lucky to Be an Octopus,*** Fiction • Narrative With Factual Content
24	Qu/qu	/kw/ as in quail on a quilt	*Living By the Sea* Families are the same in many cultures.	***Mama, Do You Love Me?,*** Fiction • Narrative ***Malia at the Beach,*** Fiction • Realistic Narrative ***Malia's Quilt,*** Fiction • Realistic Narrative
25	Uu	/ŭŭŭ/ as in upside-down	*Family Celebrations* Families are special.	***The Relatives Came,*** Fiction • Realistic Narrative ***Tall Sam,*** Fiction • Narrative
26	Xx	/ksss/ as in x on the x-ray	*School Celebrations* Learning the alphabet deserves a celebration.	***Dr. Seuss's ABC,*** Fiction • Rhyming Narrative ***The Case of the Missing X,*** Fiction • Mystery
Rev (1–26)	Aa–Zz	Review of all learned sounds	*Review* Practice makes perfect.	
Vowel Rev	a, e, i, o, u	/ăăă/, /ēēē/, /ĕĕĕ/, /īīī/, /ŏŏŏ/, /ŭŭŭ/	*Review* Do it right the first time.	***The Little Red Hen,*** Fiction • Folktale ***The Three Little Pigs,*** Fiction • Folktale

Whole Class Themes

The Whole Class themes were developed to engage the minds and imagination of young children. Kindergarten teachers are frequently heard to say, "This is the program I always wanted the time to create. We take our kids on tours of the school at the beginning of the year. We do rhyming with Dr. Seuss and do a unit on safety and healthy eating. We plant seeds in the spring and do a whole big unit on the sea. *Read Well* is a perfect fit."

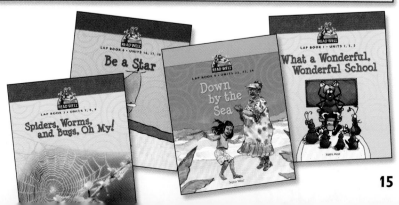

Whole Class Phonics (*continued*)

Unit Activities

I as in Insect

On a daily basis, students engage in a smorgasbord of phonics activities that focus on the newly introduced letter/sound association while simultaneously reviewing previously learned sounds. Students practice isolated letter/sound associations to build automaticity. To orally prime students for sounding out words, students stretch and shrink words. Finally, students blend sounds into words to read words, then segment words into sounds to spell words. Whole Class phonics instruction is paced to review known skills for high-performing students and preview new skills for low-performing students.

SAMPLES OF PHONICS ACTIVITIES FROM UNIT 12

Day 1

- Students rehearse all known letter/sound associations with the *Alphabet Cheer*.
- The new letter/sound focus for the unit is introduced with the *New Sound Game* and the Alphabet Poem.
- Students do Smooth and Bumpy Blending with known sounds.
- A Letter Trace activity reinforces the new letter/sound association and reviews previously learned skills.

Day 2

- Students rehearse all known letter/sound associations with the *Alphabet Cheer*.
- The new letter/sound focus for the unit is rehearsed with the Alphabet Poem.
- Students do white board dictation with known sounds.
- Students do Smooth and Bumpy Blending with known sounds.
- Students make a Letter Book during Independent Work.

> **Slow Letter**   I
>
> Capital letter I,
> Small letter i,
> I says iii.
> 12 insects in the ink,
> I, i, iii.

Research Snapshot

Phonics and Sequencing

"A program of systematic phonics instruction clearly identifies a carefully selected and useful set of letter-sound relationships and then organizes the introduction of these relationships into a logical instructional sequence" (Armbruster, Lehr, & Osborn, 2001, p. 16).

In Small Group, students learn to read at a pace just right for each individual child—not too fast and not too slow.

MASTERY-BASED INSTRUCTION

1 New Sound Introduction and Sound Review

In each unit, one new letter/sound association is introduced. Once introduced, it is reviewed daily for maintenance, using the *Read Well K* Magazines and Sound Cards.

2 Stretch and Shrink and Sound Counting

Phonemic awareness activities are included in student Magazines for ease of teaching. Spring toys are included for playful practice.

3 Smooth and Bumpy Blending, Smooth Blending, Accuracy and Fluency Building

Students learn to smoothly blend known sounds into words. Smooth Blending and the building of accuracy and fluency with pattern words leads to reading with ease and expression.

4 Tricky Words

High-frequency, irregular words are introduced gradually within the decoding sequence. For example, "was" is introduced only after students have learned the letter/sound associations for <u>w</u>, <u>a</u>, and <u>s</u>.

5 Daily Story Reading

Once words are learned, they are practiced within the context of a story. In *Read Well's* Duet Story format, students read decodable words embedded in teacher-read text. In the Solo Story format, students build fluency and independent reading skills.

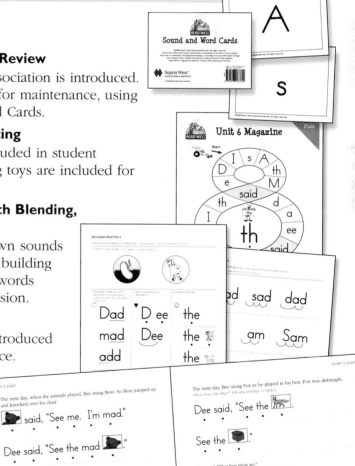

17

Small Group Phonics *(continued)*

Research Snapshot

"Sequencing helps students to learn the relationship between letters and sounds, and to use that knowledge to blend the sounds in order to read words . . . Effective programs also include books and stories that contain a lot of words for children to decode using letter-sound relationships . . . " (Vaughn & Linan-Thompson, 2004, p 31).

Read Well K Small Group
Sequence of Sounds and Themes

High-frequency sounds are introduced before low-frequency sounds.

Long vowel e as in "me" is introduced before short vowel e as in "Ed" or "engine."

Of the 100 most commonly found words in English (Fry, 2005), the long vowel e is represented in the words: he, be, we, she, and me. However, the short vowel e in only represented in the words: then, them, and get. Therefore, the long e is taught first at Unit 2, and the short vowel e is taught at Unit 19.

High-Frequency Words

By Unit 20, students have learned, within a decodable sequence, 40 of the 100 most commonly used words in English.

Easily confused letter/ sound associations are separated. For example:

• /ĭĭĭ/ is introduced at Unit 10, and /ĕĕĕ/ is introduced at Unit 19.

• /t/ is introduced at Unit 8, and /k/ is introduced at Unit 15.

Solo Stories

These fully decodable stories help students develop independence in reading.

Unit/ Prelude	Sound Sequence	Letter/Sound Association	Themes and Kinder Lessons	Unit Titles and Story Genres
Prelude A	Aa	/ăăă/ as in ant on an apple	*All About Me* It's fun to do many different things.	*Anthony Ant* Fiction • Narrative
Prelude B	I	Tricky Word: I	*Friends* Friends do many things together.	*Edith and Ann* Fiction • Narrative
Prelude C	Mm	/mmm/ as in monkey on a mountain	*Animals on the Farm* Animals can make you happy.	*The Little Farm* Fiction • Narrative
1	Ss	/sss/ as in spider in the soup	*Spider Facts and Adventures* New friends can help you feel at home in a new place.	*Spiders* Nonfiction • Expository Fiction • Narrative
2	Ee	/ēēē/ as in eel on wheels	*Eel Facts and Making Friends* Find one friend, find many more.	*All About Eels* Nonfiction • Expository Fiction • Narrative
3	Mm	/mmm/ as in monkey on a mountain	*There's No Place Like Home* After a day of adventure, home is a nice place to go.	*Monkey Business* Fiction • Narrative
4	Aa	/ăăă/ as in ant on an apple	*Insect Facts* It pays to be polite.	*Amazing Insects* Nonfiction • Expository Fiction • Narrative Fiction • Narrative
5	Dd	/d/ as in dog on a doghouse	*Dog Jobs* Dogs help people. Dogs are man's best friend.	*Man's Best Friend* Nonfiction • Expository Fiction • Narrative Fiction • Narrative
6	Th	/ththth/ as in *the*	*Rhyming Is Fun* Nicknames can be fun. Some pets are more fun than others.	*Rhyming Time* Fiction • Rhyming Narrative Fiction • Rhyming Narrative

Unit/ Prelude	Sound Sequence	Letter/Sound Association	Themes and Kinder Lessons	Unit Titles and Story Genres
7	Nn	/nnn/ as in nurse in the night	*Working on the Farm* Work hard and have fun.	*Old MacDonald's Farm* Fiction • Narrative
8	Tt	/t/ as in turtle on a tightrope	*Keep Trying* Everyone is a star.	*Turtle in the Tuba* Fiction • Narrative
9	Ww	/www/ as in worm in a wagon	*Flower Facts and Growing a Garden* Plant a seed and watch it grow.	*Flowers* Nonfiction • Expository Fiction • Narrative
10	Ii	/ĭĭĭ/ as in insect in the ink	*Families Are Special* All around the world, families help each other.	*Inuit Tales* Fiction • Narrative With Factual Content
11	Hh	/h/ as in horse in a house	*Staying Safe* Be safe and wear your life vest. Rescue workers help us in emergencies.	*Rescue Workers* Nonfiction • Narrative Fiction • Narrative Fiction • Narrative
12	Cc	/k/ as in cow on a cab	*Cat Talk* Communication and teamwork pay off.	*Cats* Nonfiction • Expository Fiction • Narrative Fiction • Narrative
13	Rr, ea	/rrr/ as in rooster on the roof; /ēēē/ as in eagle	*Be a Good Sport* Determination wins the race.	*The Race* Fiction • Narrative (adapted from an Aesop fable)
14	Sh/sh	/shshsh/ as in shells on the shore	*Family Fun* It's important and fun to do special things with your family.	*Shells on the Shore* Fiction • Narrative Fiction • Narrative
15	Kk	/k/ as in kangaroo and koala	*Kangaroo Facts* There's a special place for everyone.	*Kangaroos* Nonfiction • Expository Fiction • Narrative With Factual Content Poem
16	oo	/o͞o/ as in spoon and the moon	*Follow Your Dreams* Dreams can come true.	*Hey Diddle Diddle* Fiction • Rhyming Narrative Fiction • Narrative
17	ar	/ar/ as in star near the car	*Be Adventurous and Enjoy Your Work* When you find a job you enjoy, it's the right job for you.	*Mark and Nan Go West* Fiction • Narrative
18	Wh/wh	/wh/ as in whale in the water	*Whale Facts* Whales are interesting mammals.	*Whales* Nonfiction • Expository Fiction • Narrative Fiction • Narrative Poem
19	Ĕĕ	/ĕĕĕ/ as in Ed in the engine	*Trains Are Important* Trains move freight and help people travel long distances.	*Traveling by Train* Nonfiction • Expository Fiction • Narrative Fiction • Narrative
20	Ll	/lll/ as in lobster in the lighthouse	*Hard Work Is Rewarding* It is very important to help others.	*The Little Red Hen* Fiction • Folktale (adapted)

We can read!
We Can!
We Can!

Duet Stories

Rich in content and thematically based, these stories also include fully decodable text.

STORY 1, DUET

Kangaroo Facts

CHAPTER 1
Marsupials

This is a 🦘.

Look at the picture.
Does a kangaroo have eight legs? No, a kangaroo doesn't have eight legs. So it isn't a spider.
Does a kangaroo have six legs? No, a kangaroo doesn't have six legs. So it isn't an insect either.

STORY 1, DUET

A 🦘 is a marsupial. ... Most marsupials have ... grays in ...

Kangaroos, koalas, and opossums are all marsupials. Kangaroos, like most marsupials, live in Australia and nearby islands. They live in many different places—in the desert, grasslands, rocky hills, and sometimes even in trees!

I see a 🦘.

I think I see a 🦘
near the trees.

That 🦘 sees the 🌿.
He could eat the 🌿.

Most kangaroos sleep during the day and eat at night ...
What did you learn about kangaroos? ...
They eat plants.)

STORY 1, DUET

Kangaroos are the largest of all marsupials, sometimes growing up to seven feet tall! Kangaroos hop on their back legs to get from one place to another. Big kangaroos can hop up to 40 miles per hour. They can hop more than six feet high! A big kangaroo could hop right over a tall man.
What do you know about kangaroos? (They are very fast. They can hop very high.)

I think a 🦘 can run very fast.

I think a 🦘 can jump very high!

7

19

Whole Class and Small Group Vocabulary

Research Snapshot

Developing Vocabulary Through Repeated Exposures

After reviewing research on vocabulary, Baumann and Kame'enui (1991) concluded that words should be used "many times in many situations." Stahl (2003) explained, "As we encounter a word repeatedly, more and more information accumulates about that word until we have a vague notion of what it 'means.' As we get more information, we are able to define that word" (p. 18).

Interactive Vocabulary Lessons
Read Well uses selected words "many times in many situations."

VOCABULARY DEVELOPMENT OF . . . *adventure*

What's a story without adventure? In *Read Well K*, "adventure" and other content-related words are taught explicitly in both Small Group and Whole Class, giving students multiple exposures to words rich in meaning.

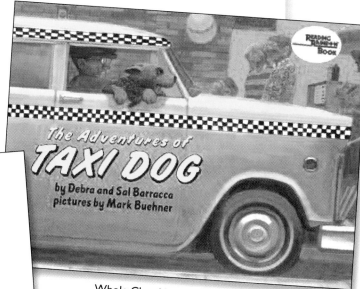

Whole Class Unit 11 Literature Selection

STORY 3, DUET

Sahale's Adventure

What's the title of the story? (Sahale's Adventure)
An *adventure* is doing something or going somewhere new and interesting.
What do you think Sahale will do in this story?

CHAPTER 1
Sahale Travels With the Wind

Sahale was a little spider who lived in a very big and noisy city. She dreamed of going on an adventure. She wanted to visit the country with its trees and big meadows. Sahale left her old web and crawled down the waterspout.

Touch Sahale. Where do you think she is going?

Touch under the first big word and read.

"I the busy city. I hear the busy city.

I want to visit the country. I want to visit a farm."

What does Sahale want? (to visit the country, visit a farm)
Yes, she wants to do something new and interesting. She wants to go on an adventure.

Read Well's unique Duet Story format provides an opportunity to develop students' listening and speaking vocabulary—even as students read only decodable text.

VOCABULARY DEVELOPMENT OF . . . communicate

In Small Group Unit 12, students are introduced to the vocabulary word "communicate," first to develop receptive language.

Introducing Vocabulary

There are many ways to talk to one another.
Show me a sad face.
Sometimes you can talk, or *communicate*, with others by showing how you feel.
You are showing me a sad feeling.

Show me a happy face.
You are talking, or communicating, by showing how you feel. You are showing me a happy feeling.
Look at the picture. Who do you think will be communicating in this story?

STUDENT-FRIENDLY DEFINITIONS are provided in the teacher's guides. Scripting provides a model for explaining a new word by making connections with what children already know.

Whole Class Read Alouds and Small Group Story Reading provide many opportunities for deepening word knowledge.

VOCABULARY DEVELOPMENT OF . . . communicate

In Whole Class Unit 19, students deepen their understanding of the word "communicate" when they hear the Lap Book story "Bee Facts" and learn that bees talk to each other.

One of the ways bee talk to each other is by waggling their bodies. This is called the waggle dance.
Everybody, let's waggle our bodies. The waggle dance is how bees *communicate*, or tell each other things.
When a bee waggles its body, it is . . . communicating.

The waggle dance communicates where to find the food.
Help me tell that fact. The waggle dance . . .
communicates where to find the food.

Whole Class Comprehension

Research Snapshot

Read Alouds

Researchers tend to agree that the features of an effective Read Aloud are "focusing discussion on the major story ideas, dealing with ideas as they are encountered in contrast to after the entire story has been read, and involving children in the discussion with opportunities to be reflective" (Beck & McKeown, 2001, p. 11).

A Comprehension Walk Through Unit 5

On Day 1, each unit features a children's literature selection that spotlights the unit theme. Art Projects enhance discussions and sometimes provide props for students to use during story readings. On Days 2 and 3, students hear the interactive *Read Well* Lap Book stories written specifically to build important connections with the literature centerpiece and theme. Finally, students retell the stories with Pocket Chart Cards, make retell books, and then retell their stories to friends and families at home.

STORY ELEMENTS
Students identify the action and then act it out.

Day 1: Read Aloud • Lit Book

Read the classic folktale *Caps for Sale*, in which mischievous monkeys steal a peddler's caps. While reading *Caps for Sale*, you will guide interaction and keep students focused on the important events of the story.

The peddler wanted the monkey to give him back his caps.

So what did the peddler do?
(stamped his feet)
While he stamped his feet, the peddler said,
"You give be back my . . . (caps)."

Everyone, stamp your feet and say
"You give me back my caps!"
(You give me back my caps!)

CAPS FOR SALE
A Tale of a Peddler, Some Monkeys and Their Monkey Business

TOLD & ILLUSTRATED BY
Esphyr Slobodkina

Day 1: Art Project • Straw Hat

Following the Read Aloud, children make straw hats. The Art Project creates an opportunity to make connections with the story and to build vocabulary knowledge.

VOCABULARY

Students begin learning about synonyms with simple words.

What did the peddler wear on his head? (a cap)

What do you wear on your head? (a hat)

Cap is another word for *hat*.

Put on a completed sample of the Art Project.

Do you wear hats that look like this?

Show a hat typical of those worn in your community.

What do our hats do for us?

(keep us warm; keep us dry . . .)

Tomorrow, we're going to read a story about straw hats.

Straw hats do not keep people warm.

They protect people from the hot sun.

We're going to make straw hats, so we can act out a story.

Days 2 and 3: Read Aloud • Lap Book

The Lap Book story "Straw Hats for Sale" is an adaptation of *Caps for Sale*. Mischievous monkeys steal an old Japanese woman's hats and won't give them back.

While reading the story, students participate by acting out what happened.

Everyone, what did the little old woman say? (Give me back my hats.)

Shake your finger and say that with me. (Give me back my hats.)

What do you think the monkeys will do?

When the old woman isn't able to get her hats back, like all polite Japanese people, the old woman bows her head.

PREDICTIONS

Students make predictions based on knowledge built in the program.

What do you think the monkeys will do next?

What do you think will happen if we bow? (Our hats will fall off.)

Everyone, bow.

That's just what the monkeys did, and their hats fell to the ground.

CAUSE AND EFFECT

At the conclusion of the story, students pretend to be monkeys, wearing their own straw hats.

Day 3: Pocket Chart Retell and Retell Book

Students retell the story and sequence story pictures, using Pocket Chart Cards. Then they make their own retell books, so they can tell the story over and over again to friends and relatives.

Whole Class Comprehension (*continued*)

Read Well includes comprehension objectives that tap the thought processes from *A Taxonomy for Learning, Teaching and Assessing: A Revision of Bloom's Taxonomy of Educational Objectives* (Anderson, Krathwohl, Airasian, Cruikshank, Mayer, Pintrich, Raths, & Wittrock, 2000). Because specific objectives frequently cross categories, objectives are listed by what students do—predict, identify, infer, etc.—as well as by the broader categories of higher-order thinking. These thought processes build knowledge in the areas of facts, concepts, procedural knowledge, and metacognitive knowledge.

Read Well K Whole Class Comprehension Objectives

Thought Processes	1	2	3	4	5	6	7	8	9	R	10	11	12	13	14	15	16	17	18	E	19	20	21	22	23	24	25	26	R	VR
Remember	x	x	x	x	x	x	x	x	x	x	x	x	x	x	x	x	x	x	x	x	x	x	x	x	x	x	x	x	x	x
Understand	x	x	x	x	x	x	x	x	x	x	x	x	x	x	x	x	x	x	x	x	x	x	x	x	x	x	x	x	x	x
Apply	x	x	x	x	x	x	x	x	x	x	x	x	x	x	x	x	x	x	x	x	x	x	x	x	x	x	x	x	x	x
Analyze													x				x													
Evaluate	x	x	x	x	x	x	x	x	x	x	x	x	x	x	x	x	x	x	x	x	x	x	x	x	x	x	x	x	x	x
Create																	x						x		x					

Objectives	1	2	3	4	5	6	7	8	9	R	10	11	12	13	14	15	16	17	18	E	19	20	21	22	23	24	25	26	R	VR
Priming Background Knowledge		x		x	x	x	x	x	x	x	x	x	x	x			x	x	x	x	x	x	x	x		x				x
Building Knowledge	x	x	x			x	x	x	x	x	x	x	x	x	x	x	x		x	x	x		x	x	x	x	x	x	x	x
Making Connections	x	x	x	x	x	x	x	x	x	x	x	x	x	x	x	x	x	x	x	x	x	x	x	x	x	x	x	x	x	x
Dramatizing	x	x	x		x	x	x	x	x		x	x	x	x		x	x	x	x	x	x	x	x	x	x	x	x	x	x	x
Illustrating							x	x	x	x	x	x	x				x	x	x	x	x	x	x	x	x	x	x		x	x
Predicting	x	x	x	x	x	x	x	x	x	x	x	x	x	x	x	x	x	x	x	x	x	x	x	x	x	x	x	x	x	x
Identifying	x	x	x	x	x	x	x	x	x	x	x	x	x	x	x	x	x	x	x	x	x	x	x	x	x	x	x	x	x	x
Describing	x	x					x		x	x	x			x	x	x	x	x	x			x	x		x	x	x			
Demonstrating	x	x	x	x			x	x		x			x	x		x	x		x	x	x	x		x	x	x	x		x	
Defining	x	x	x	x	x	x	x		x		x	x	x	x	x	x	x	x	x	x	x	x	x	x	x	x	x	x	x	x
Explaining	x		x	x	x	x	x	x	x	x	x	x	x	x	x	x	x	x	x	x	x	x	x	x	x	x	x	x	x	x
Inferring	x		x	x	x	x	x	x	x	x	x	x	x	x	x	x	x	x	x	x	x	x	x	x	x	x	x	x	x	x
Classifying	x	x	x	x	x	x	x	x	x	x	x	x			x	x		x	x			x				x				x
Comparing													x					x								x				
Responding	x	x	x	x	x	x	x	x	x	x	x	x	x	x	x	x	x	x	x	x	x	x	x	x	x	x	x	x	x	x
Visualizing					x												x													
Questioning																									x				x	
Summarizing				x			x	x	x	x	x	x		x	x	x	x	x	x	x	x	x	x	x	x	x	x	x	x	x
Sequencing				x			x	x				x		x	x	x	x	x		x	x	x	x	x	x	x		x		x
Making Judgments														x	x	x				x		x			x		x			x
Generating Ideas																x						x								

Small Group Comprehension

Research Snapshot

Comprehension

"Research shows that teacher questioning strongly supports and advances students' learning from reading. Questions appear to be effective for improving learning from reading because they:

• give students a purpose for reading
• help students to monitor their comprehension
• focus students' attention on what they are to learn
• help students to review content and relate what they have learned to what they already know"

(Armbruster, Lehr, & Osborn, 2001, p. 51).

From Unit 1, *Read Well K's* Duet Story format engages students in meaningful text.

From Unit 1, student attention is focused on predicting what will happen and identifying important story elements—main character, problem, goal, action, and solution.

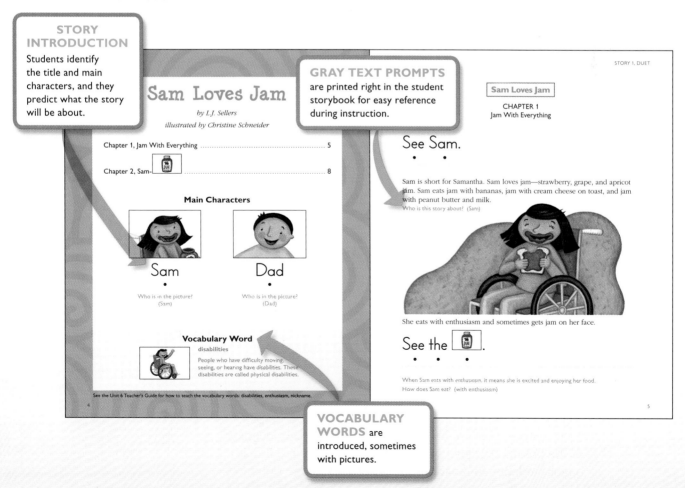

STORY INTRODUCTION
Students identify the title and main characters, and they predict what the story will be about.

GRAY TEXT PROMPTS are printed right in the student storybook for easy reference during instruction.

STORY 1, DUET

Sam Loves Jam
by L.J. Sellers
illustrated by Christine Schneider

Chapter 1, Jam With Everything 5

Chapter 2, Sam-[JAM] 8

Main Characters

Sam   Dad

Who is in the picture?   Who is in the picture?
(Sam)   (Dad)

Vocabulary Word
disabilities
People who have difficulty moving, seeing, or hearing have *disabilities*. These disabilities are called physical disabilities.

See the Unit 6 Teacher's Guide for how to teach the vocabulary words: disabilities, enthusiasm, nickname.

4

Sam Loves Jam

CHAPTER 1
Jam With Everything

See Sam.
• •

Sam is short for Samantha. Sam loves jam—strawberry, grape, and apricot jam. Sam eats jam with bananas, jam with cream cheese on toast, and jam with peanut butter and milk.
Who is this story about? (Sam)

She eats with enthusiasm and sometimes gets jam on her face.

See the [JAM].
• • •

When Sam eats with *enthusiasm*, it means she is excited and enjoying her food.
How does Sam eat? (with enthusiasm)

5

VOCABULARY WORDS are introduced, sometimes with pictures.

Research Snapshot

Story Structure and Summarizing

To develop comprehension strategies in the early units, *Read Well* embeds questions that direct children to the central content of the story (as recommended by Beck, Omanson, & McKeown, 1982). Stories are then orally retold within a scaffolded story summary process. As students progress through the program, these strategies prepare children for written story mapping, which Baumann and Bergeron (1993) found to increase young children's comprehension.

Higher-Order Thinking and Summarization

Small Group Unit 6 Storybook

Animal House

CHAPTER 1
The New Pet

There was an old woman who lived in a shoe. She had so many pets she didn't know what to do. One day the woman brought home another pet. This time, the woman named Dee brought home a bee.

"See the [bee]," said Dee.

"Bee will live here too."
Bear, who liked to sit in a chair, looked quite distraught. "That just won't do," said Bear.
"Nonsense," said Dee. "I love that bee."

Who is the story about? (an old woman named Dee)
She had so many pets she didn't know what to do. What was her problem? (She had too many pets.)
Yes, she had too many pets, but she brought home a bee. What do you think will happen next?

STORY 3, DUET

The next day, when the animals played, Bee stung Bear. So Bear jumped up and knocked over his chair.

[Bear] said, "See me. I'm mad."

Dee said, "See the mad [bear]."

"That's not funny," s[...]
"Nonsense,"

said Dee. "[...]

Why did Bear get mad? (He[...])
That's a problem. Have you [...]
Were you distraught?

THINKING ALOUD

Making Connections, Predicting
After students make their predictions, say something like:

Yes, bees can sting. I think [José] might be right. Dee's shoe-house is so crowded the bee might get mad and sting the other animals.

But then, perhaps [Sandy] will be right. A bee is small. Perhaps they will all live happily ever after.

Story Summary

Animal House

Who is the story about?

Dee

● At the beginning of the story, Dee brought home a pet bee to live with the other animals.
What did Dee do? (brought home a pet bee)

■ In the middle of the story, Bee stung Bear and Fox.
What did Bee do? (Bee stung Bear and Fox.)
What did Dee do? (nothing)

■ Who did Bee sting next? (Bee stung Skunk.)
What happened after that? (Skunk made the house stink.)

▲ At the end, Dee opened a window.
What did Dee do? (Bee flew away.)
How did the other animals feel? (happy)
How did Dee feel? (sad)
Do you think she was distraught?

Easy-to-reference ant notes in the teacher's guides model how to think aloud with children as they engage in critical comprehension processes. Gray-text questions in the student Storybooks guide discussions so that comprehension strategies are purposefully developed, even as instructors are busily attending to the many needs of the group. Narrative stories end with a story retell that builds students' summarization and oral language skills.

Small Group comprehension objectives also tap the thought processes from *A Taxonomy for Learning, Teaching and Assessing: A Revision of Bloom's Taxonomy of Educational Objectives* (Anderson et al., 2000).

Read Well K Small Group Comprehension Objectives

Thought Processes	A	B	C	1	2	3	4	5	6	7	8	9	10	11	12	13	14	15	16	17	18	19	20
Remember	x	x	x	x	x	x	x	x	x	x	x	x	x	x	x	x	x	x	x	x	x	x	x
Understand	x	x	x	x	x	x	x	x	x	x	x	x	x	x	x	x	x	x	x	x	x	x	x
Apply				x	x	x	x	x	x	x	x	x	x	x	x	x	x	x	x	x	x	x	x
Evaluate				x						x		x	x					x	x			x	x
Create										x									x		x		

Objectives	A	B	C	1	2	3	4	5	6	7	8	9	10	11	12	13	14	15	16	17	18	19	20
Priming Background Knowledge			x	x			x			x	x	x	x	x	x			x			x		
Building Knowledge										x		x	x				x	x			x	x	
Making Connections	x	x	x	x			x	x		x	x	x	x	x	x	x	x	x	x		x	x	x
Dramatizing		x				x	x		x	x	x										x		
Predicting		x	x	x	x	x	x	x	x	x	x	x	x	x	x	x	x	x	x	x	x	x	x
Identifying	x	x	x	x	x	x	x	x	x	x	x	x	x	x	x	x	x	x	x	x	x	x	x
Describing				x												x	x	x	x		x		x
Defining				x	x	x	x	x	x	x	x	x	x	x	x	x	x	x		x	x	x	x
Explaining		x	x	x	x	x	x	x	x	x	x	x	x	x	x	x	x	x	x	x	x	x	x
Inferring	x	x	x	x	x	x	x	x	x	x	x	x	x	x	x	x	x	x	x	x	x	x	x
Classifying																		x				x	
Comparing																				x			
Responding				x							x		x	x				x	x			x	x
Visualizing													x		x								
Summarizing	x	x	x															x				x	x
Generating Ideas										x								x			x		

27

Whole Class and Small Group Genres

Research Snapshot

Building Knowledge

"Domain knowledge, the most recently understood principle, increases fluency, broadens vocabulary, and enables deeper comprehension. If relevant knowledge is lacking, conscious comprehension strategies cannot activate it" (Hirsch, 2003, p. 12).

Things That Creep, Crawl, Buzz, and Breach!

Read Well K **Whole Class and Small Group include nonfiction expository text selections and narratives with factual content.**

WHOLE CLASS TEACHER-READ NONFICTION TITLES

Literature

Unit 8: Wonderful Worms

Unit 23: Gentle Giant Octopus

Lap Books

Unit 6: Friendship

Unit 7: Spider Facts

Unit 8: Earthworm Facts

Unit 11: Helping Dogs

Unit 12: Insect Facts

Unit 19: Bee Facts

Unit 20: Flower Facts

SMALL GROUP STUDENT-READ NONFICTION TITLES

Unit 1: Spider Facts

Unit 2: Eel Facts

Unit 4: Insect Facts

Unit 5: Dogs With Jobs

Unit 9: Flower Facts

Unit 11: Rescue Workers on the Job

Unit 12: Cat Talk

Unit 15: Kangaroo Facts

Unit 18: What Is a Whale?

Unit 19: Trains

Unit 19 Lap Book

Unit 18 Storybook

Unit 4 Storybook

Fluent Reading

Reading fluency is recognized by researchers as an essential element of comprehension (Adams, 1990; National Reading Panel, 2000; Samuels & Flor, 1997). Hirsch (2003) explains, "A person who reads fast has 'automated' many of the underlying processes involved in reading, and can, therefore, devote conscious attention to textual meaning rather than to the processes themselves" (p. 12).

Fluent reading is accurate and expressive.

Accurate Reading

Fully decodable text allows children to apply their skills with accuracy. *Read Well* students confidently read passages of gradually increasing difficulty.

Expressive Reading

After reading text for accuracy and comprehension, students practice expressive reading with Short Passage practice. First, they listen to the teacher read. Then, they read with the teacher, and, finally, they read the passage individually.

Short Passage Practice

- Demonstrate expressive accurate reading of the first few sentences. Read at a pace slightly faster than students' reading rate. Say something like:

  Follow with your finger while I read with expression.

  "See me in a tree," said {Koala}.

  "This is neat. I can eat and eat treats in this seat."

- Guide practice with your voice.

  Let's read the sentences together. "See me in a tree," said {Koala}. "This . . ."

- Provide individual turns.

  [Nancy], please read the sentences. ("See me in a tree," said {Koala}. "This . . .")

Fluent Reading

To build the fluency needed for comprehension, students engage in repeated readings of their Solo Stories. Students choral read stories, engage in Short Passage Practice, Whisper Read while others are doing Timed Readings, Partner Read, and take Solo Stories home to share with their parents.

Assessing Fluency

Fluency is assessed at the end of each unit, beginning with Unit 6. Ongoing progress monitoring ensures that students receive the instruction and practice they need to be successful.

Extra Practice

Additional fluency practice is provided in each unit's optional Extra Practice pages.

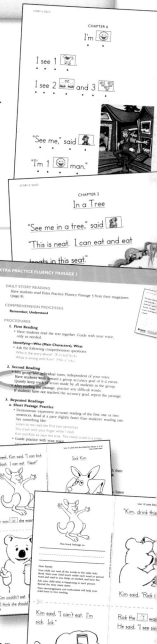

Read Well's All-Inclusive Framework

Research Snapshot

Tailored to Fit

"At all grade levels, but particularly in kindergarten and the early grades, children are known to vary greatly in the skills they bring to school . . . Teachers should be able to assess the needs of the individual students and tailor instruction to meet specific needs . . . In light of this, teachers need to be flexible in their phonics instruction in order to adapt it to individual student needs" (National Reading Panel, 2000, p. 11).

Read Well K's all-inclusive framework meets the needs of all young children—from intervention to acceleration.

Each school can tailor the program to the needs of children. *Read Well K* includes:

WHOLE CLASS ACTIVITIES

Young children benefit from interaction with other children of diverse abilities, interests, and backgrounds. *Read Well K* encourages teachers to engage in Whole Class literacy activities to provide a shared literacy experience for all children. *Read Well K* Whole Class activities support and enhance the skills and content learned in Small Group instruction.

SMALL GROUP INSTRUCTION

Children need to feel comfortable and competent as they learn to read. Instruction in small groups, based on mastery of skills, allows students to become readers at a pace appropriate to their development. Students establish essential reading foundations during Small Group instruction.

INDIVIDUAL ASSESSMENT AND PRACTICE

The voices of individual children can be lost in a group, so it's important that all children have opportunities to share their accomplishments one-to-one with supportive adults. *Read Well K* includes individualized assessments at the end of each unit to ensure that every child's needs are being met. When needed, multiple options for independent practice can be implemented.

Position Statement

Developmentally Appropriate

The International Reading Association and the National Association for the Education of Young Children (1998) believe that "goals and expectations for young children's achievement in reading and writing should be developmentally appropriate; that is, challenging but achievable, with sufficient adult support" (p. 15).

Small Group lessons provide:

❶ Appropriate Placement

Using the *Read Well K* placement test as a guide, students are placed in small groups with similar skill levels. Placement procedures include multiple entry points. Thus, students begin in *Read Well K* based on their prior knowledge.

❷ Continuous Progress Monitoring

The progress of each child is then carefully monitored so that instruction is tailored to the mastery-based needs of each student.

❸ Individual and Group Prescriptions

Each unit includes guidelines for accelerating, maintaining, or providing additional practice to achieve mastery. Groups are fluid because the needs of children vary across time.

❹ Extra Practice

Each unit includes three or four Extra Practice lessons for students who need additional instruction and practice to build deeper levels of mastery.

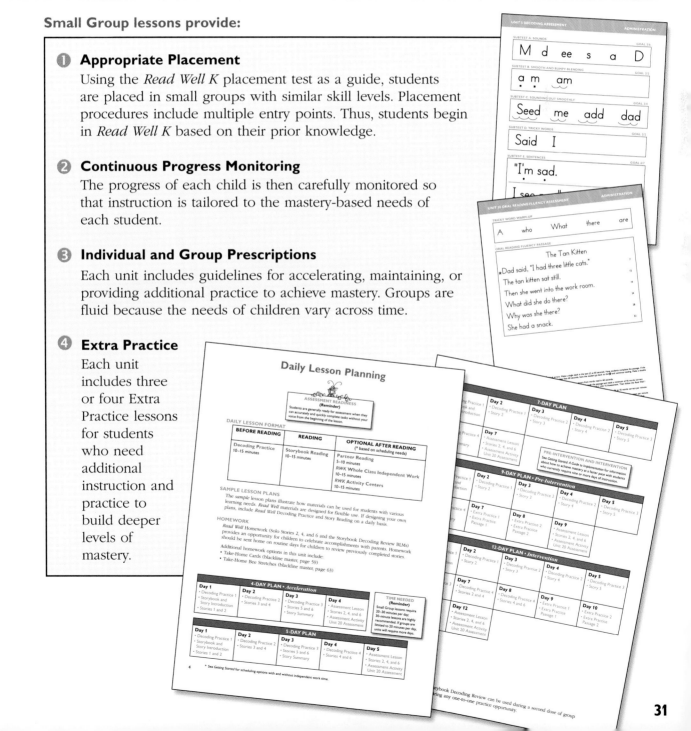

Unique Instructional Design

Meeting the Needs of All Kids:
A Core Program With Built-In Intervention and Acceleration

Read Well's elegantly interwoven instructional design enables struggling students to reach benchmark, average students to exceed expectations, and high performers to excel.

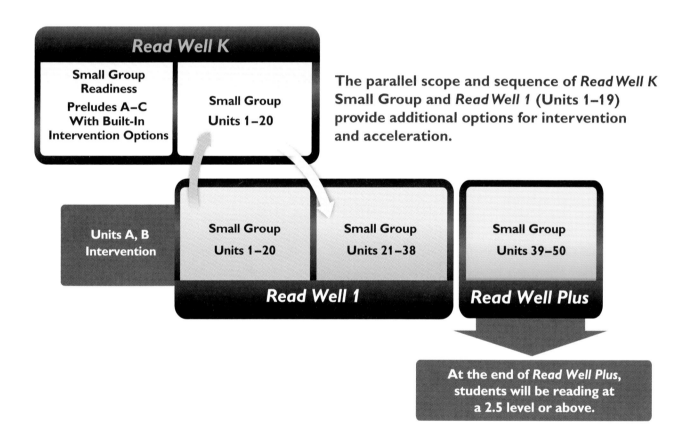

Read Well K

Small Group Readiness Preludes A–C With Built-In Intervention Options	Small Group Units 1–20

The parallel scope and sequence of *Read Well K* Small Group and *Read Well 1* (Units 1–19) provide additional options for intervention and acceleration.

Units A, B Intervention	Small Group Units 1–20	Small Group Units 21–38	Small Group Units 39–50

Read Well 1

Read Well Plus

At the end of *Read Well Plus*, students will be reading at a 2.5 level or above.

Placement testing gives you appropriate starting points in *Read Well* for all kindergarten, first grade, and remedial second and third grade students.

Learning is always challenging but achievable.

Whole Class Materials for Morning Routines

Whole Class Program Guide: *Getting Started*

- Program Overview
- Getting the Year Started: Scheduling, the First Few Weeks of School, Teaching Behavioral Expectations
- Teaching *Read Well* Whole Class
- Alphabet Routines
- Read Alouds and Related Activities
- Independent Work
- Language Priming
- Appendix: Setting Up and Organizing Materials; Scope and Sequence Word Lists, Blackline Masters

Whole Class Teacher's Guides

6 full-color, teacher-friendly, spiral-bound teacher's guides, providing detailed instruction for 30 five-day units

Includes:

- Daily Lesson Planning
- Objectives
- Instructions for Alphabet Routines, Read Alouds, Independent Work

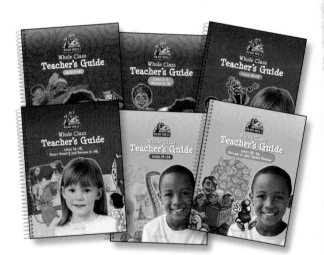

Lap Book Set

9 casebound books containing theme-related stories for whole class reading (10 x 12)

Teaches and Supports:

Concepts of Print, Comprehension, Vocabulary

Whole Class Materials

Children's Literature Set

26 children's literature favorites

Teaches and Supports:

Vocabulary, Comprehension

ABC Poem Posters

27 full-color posters

Teaches and Supports:

Oral Language, Phonemic Awareness (beginning sound), Phonics, Phonological

ABC Wall Cards

Double-sided letter cards, with and without pictures, *available in plain or slanted text*

Teaches and Supports:

Oral Language, Phonemic Awareness (beginning sound), Alphabetic Knowledge, Phonics

CD of Songs

Alphabet Cheer, Alphabet Songs

Teaches and Supports:

Oral Language, Phonemic Awareness (beginning sound), Alphabetic Knowledge, Phonics, Music Experience

Whole Class Blending Cards

50 Smooth and Bumpy Blending cards (8½ x 11)

Teaches and Supports:

Oral Language, Phonemic Awareness, Phonics

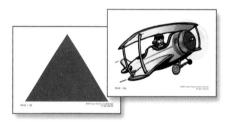

Pocket Chart Cards

181 full-color picture cards

Teaches and Supports:

Oral Language, Concepts of Print, Phonemic Awareness, Phonics, Fluency, Conventions, Comprehension, Vocabulary

Independent Work—*My Activity Books 1–3*

- *My Activity Books* are consumable; blackline masters also included in the instructor's package; *available in plain or slanted text*

- Independent Work blackline masters include Letter Trace, Letter Books, Bookmaking, Sorting, Sentence Writing, Jigsaw Puzzles, Sentence Scrambles, and Little Books—providing at least one activity per day for students.

Teaches and Supports:

Independent Work Habits, Oral Language, Concepts of Print, Phonemic Awareness, Phonics, Handwriting, Comprehension, Vocabulary, Fluency, Fine Motor Skills

Whole Class Activities

- Blackline masters; *available in plain or slanted text*

- Whole Class activities include optional Homework, Art Projects, and ABC Scrapbook Art for most units.

Teaches and Supports:

Oral Language, Phonemic Awareness, Alphabetic Knowledge, Phonics, Handwriting, Comprehension, Vocabulary, Fine Motor Skills

Small Group Materials for Mastery-Based Instruction

Small Group Program Guide: *Getting Started*

- Program Overview
- Getting the Year Started: Scheduling, The First Few Weeks of School, Behavioral Expectations
- Small Group Lesson Planning: Daily Lesson Planning Differentiated Plans, Lesson Planning Supplies, Double Dosing
- Small Group Decoding Practice
- Small Group Story Reading
- End of the Unit: Assessments, Making Decisions
- Blackline Masters
- Scope and Sequence Word Lists

Small Group Teacher's Guides

Bound by unit for ease of sharing (Preludes A–C and Units 1–20)

Includes:

- Important Tips
- Daily Lesson Planning
- Objectives
- Instructions for Decoding Practice (Magazines), Story Reading, Assessments, and Extra Practice
- Extra Practice blackline masters: Lessons, Games, and Fluency Passages

Teacher's Storybooks

2 enlarged Storybooks (including Magazines) for Units 1 and 2

Supports:

Vocabulary, Comprehension, Fluency, Guided Practice with the whole class

Small Group Blending Cards

40 smooth and bumpy blending cards
(8½ x 11)

Teaches and Supports:

Oral Language, Phonemic Awareness,
(Blending and Segmenting), Phonics

Sound and Word Cards

100 sound and word cards (8½ x 11)

Teaches and Supports:

Phonics (Letter/Sound Fluency),
Irregular Words

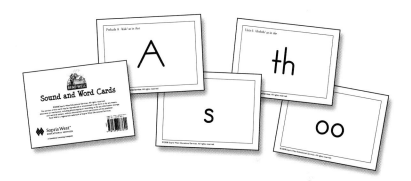

Assessment Manual

Key Content

- Instructions for placing students
- Instructions for assessing students
- Instructions for flexible grouping, diagnostic
  prescriptions, and Jell-Well Reviews
- Blackline masters: Placement Inventory,
  Decoding and Fluency Assessments, Student
  and Group Assessment Records

Student Magazines: Preludes A–C and Units 1–20

(*consumable; available in plain or slanted text*)

Teaches and Supports:

Concepts of Print, Oral Language, Phonemic
Awareness, Phonics, Comprehension, Vocabulary,
Handwriting

Small Group Materials *(continued)*

Student Storybooks

(nonconsumable)

20 full-color Storybooks containing Duet and Solo Stories

Teaches and Supports:

Vocabulary, Comprehension, Fluency

Assessment Activities Set

Blackline masters for Independent Work activities done while other students are being assessed

Teaches and Supports:

Phonics, Handwriting, Fine Motor Skills, Comprehension, Conventions

Homework

Blackline masters

Teaches and Supports:

Fluency, Comprehension, Family Connections

Manipulatives

Used With and Supports:

Games and activities

Getting the Year Started

In this section:

2.1 Scheduling

2.2 The First Few Weeks of School

2.3 Tips for Teaching
Behavioral Expectations

Section 2.1

Scheduling

Position Statement

Wide Range of Literacy Skills

". . . it is common to find within a kindergarten classroom, a 5-year range in children's literacy-related skills and functioning (Riley, 1996). What this means is that some kindergarteners may have skills characteristic of the typical 3-year-old, while others might be functioning at the level of a typical 8-year-old" (NAEYC and IRA, 1998, p 5).

Scheduling Options

Not only do kindergarten children come to school with a range of skills, kindergarten programs across the country vary tremendously. For example, students may attend:

- Full-day programs, five days per week
- Half-time programs, five half days per week
- Half-time programs, with two full days one week and three full days the next week.

Some programs may have full-time instructional assistants, while others have part-time help or none at all. Not all classrooms are created equal either—ranging from 15–32 students. As with all programs, ease of implementation is dependent on time, collaboration, and administrative support.

Read Well's mastery-based Small Group instruction is crucial to reading success. Though challenging to schedule, ideal Small Group instruction provides each child with:

- 30 minutes of instruction per group, per day
- Five days of instruction per week, per group
- Four groups per class
- Minimal grouping between classrooms
- A second dose of instruction for the lowest-performing students

Keeping all that in mind, we've created various scheduling scenarios to help you fit *Read Well* Whole Class and Small Group into your busy school day.

Recommended Plan, Instructional Teams

Through collaboration and administrative support, a half hour per day is set aside in which all children are comfortably instructed in small groups. Groups can be taught by trained kindergarten teachers, assistants, and others—reading teachers, Title I teachers, administrators, counselors, and librarians.

The following scenario shows how a half-day kindergarten program might be scheduled. If you have a full day, these time periods can be expanded—or left as is, giving you the afternoon free for other activities.

Sample Schedule	
8:45–9:00	Entering Routine: *Read Well* Independent Work and Math
9:00–9:20	Morning Opening: *Read Well* Alphabet Routines, Calendar Math
9:20–9:35	*Read Well* Read Aloud and Pocket Chart Activity
9:35–10:00	*Read Well* Small Group Instruction (all students in teacher-directed small groups)
10:00–10:30	Specials Rotation: Day 1—Library; Day 2—PE; Day 3—Computers; Day 4—PE; Day 5—Music
10:30–11:00	Math
11:00–11:20	*Read Well* Activities Rotation: Day 1—Art Project; Day 2—White Boards; Day 3—Choice/Journals; Day 4—Scrapbook; Day 5—White Boards
11:20–11:30	*Read Well* Songs, Stretch and Shrink, Smooth and Bumpy Blending

Special Note: Most Art Project, Scrapbook, and Journal activities are optional—providing time for you to integrate other activities, choice time, etc.

With a full-day program, the schedule can be more leisurely!

Scheduling • Scenario 2

Teacher and a Specialist or Assistant (1 Hour)

A specialist or assistant is available to teach two, 20–30 minute Small Group rotations. During the first rotation, two groups work independently while you and the other instructor teach groups. This is repeated for a second rotation.

The following scenario shows how a half-day kindergarten program might be scheduled. If you have a full day, these time periods can be expanded—or left as is, giving you the afternoon free for other activities.

Sample Schedule		
8:45–9:00	Entering Routine: Math Work	
9:00–9:15	Morning Opening and *Read Well* Alphabet Routines	
9:15–9:30	*Read Well* Read Aloud and Pocket Chart Activity	
	Groups 1 and 2	**Groups 3 and 4**
9:30–9:50 (20 minutes)	**Teacher/Assistant Directed** *Read Well* Decoding Practice *Read Well* Story Reading	**Independent Work** *Read Well* Partner Reading *Read Well* Whole Class Independent Work *Read Well K* Activity Centers (Instructor: One-to-one checkouts and assessments)
9:50–10:20	Specials Rotation: Day 1—Library; Day 2—PE; Day 3—Computers; Day 4—PE; Day 5—Music	
10:20–10:45	Math	
	Groups 3 and 4	**Groups 1 and 2**
10:45–11:05 (20 minutes)	**Teacher/Assistant Directed** *Read Well* Decoding Practice *Read Well* Story Reading	**Independent Work** *Read Well* Partner Reading *Read Well* Whole Class Independent Work *Read Well K* Activity Centers (Instructor: One-to-one checkouts and assessments)
11:05–11:25	*Read Well* Activities Rotation: Day 1—Art Project; Day 2—White Boards; Day 3—Choice/Journals; Day 4—Scrapbook; Day 5—White Boards	
11:25–11:30	*Read Well* Songs, Stretch and Shrink, Smooth and Bumpy Blending	

Reminder: Most Art Project, Scrapbook, and Journal activities are optional—providing time for you to integrate other activities, choice time, etc.

Teacher and Specialist or Assistant (½ Hour)

A specialist or assistant is available to teach one, 20–30 minute Small Group rotation. The group is divided into three groups (rather than four). The lowest-performing group receives instruction five days per week, while the middle- and highest-performing groups receive Small Group instruction every other day.

The following scenario shows how a half-day kindergarten program might be scheduled. If you have a full day, these time periods can be expanded—or left as is, giving you the afternoon free for other activities.

Sample Schedule	
8:45–9:00	Entering Routine: Math Work/*Read Well* Independent Work
9:00–9:20	Morning Opening: *Read Well* Alphabet Routines and Math Routines
9:20–9:35	*Read Well* Read Aloud and Pocket Chart Activity
9:35–10:00	*Read Well* Small Group Rotation Group 1 receives instruction five days per week. Groups 2 and 3 receive instruction every other day.
10:00–10:30	Specials Rotation: Day 1—Library; Day 2—PE; Day 3—Computers; Day 4—PE; Day 5—Music
10:30–11:00	Math
11:00–11:20	*Read Well* Activities Rotation: Day 1—Art Project; Day 2—White Boards; Day 3—Choice/Journals; Day 4—Scrapbook; Day 5—White Boards
11:20–11:30	*Read Well* Songs, Stretch and Shrink, Smooth and Bumpy Blending

Reminder: Most Art Project, Scrapbook, and Journal activities are optional—providing time for you to integrate other activities.

Note: If you do not have instructional assistance for a half hour per day, your options for providing individually appropriate instruction are limited.

The First Few Weeks of School

During this important time, classroom teachers help young children feel welcome, safe, and comfortable. Classroom routines are established and behavioral expectations are taught. In addition to developing each child's sense of security, the first few weeks are also a critical time to begin establishing kindergarten literacy foundations.

Placement Testing

Under ideal conditions, an assessment team of specialists and assistants completes the placement testing during the first two weeks of school. Students will place in Prelude A to get ready for formal reading instruction, or they will begin formal reading instruction at *RWK* Unit 1, 6, 10, 16 or at *RW1* Unit 21 or higher. Students are placed into groups based on their prior knowledge. Once instruction begins, group membership changes often.

If an assessment team is not available, classroom teachers should assess a few students each day.

Whole Class Instruction

Unit 1 is a welcoming unit, complete with name games and school tours that can be implemented in either the first or second week of school.

Read Well K Whole Class is composed of 30 five-day units. With 36 weeks of school, this allows flexibility for special holidays, parent conferences, and field trips. If your school has a half-time kindergarten program, this allows you to run six-day units.

Units 1–3 are designed to acquaint children with their new setting and friends. Take a tour of your school and meet special people. Teach children how to work independently. By Unit 4, many teachers and students are ready to add Small Group instruction.

Behavioral Expectations

During the first few weeks of school, classroom teachers should focus on teaching students how to behave responsibly during these times:

- Circle activities
- When transitioning from Whole Class activities to Independent Work or Small Group instruction
- When working independently
- When transitioning from one classroom to another (Walk-to-Read)

(See Tips for Teaching Behavioral Expectations, page 46.)

Starting Small Groups

Small Group instruction begins after:

- Working out scheduling options
- Administering the *Read Well* Placement Inventory
- Completing Whole Class Unit 4 and before completing Whole Class Unit 9 (With each year of experience implementing the program, kindergarten teachers tend to start Small Group instruction a little earlier.)

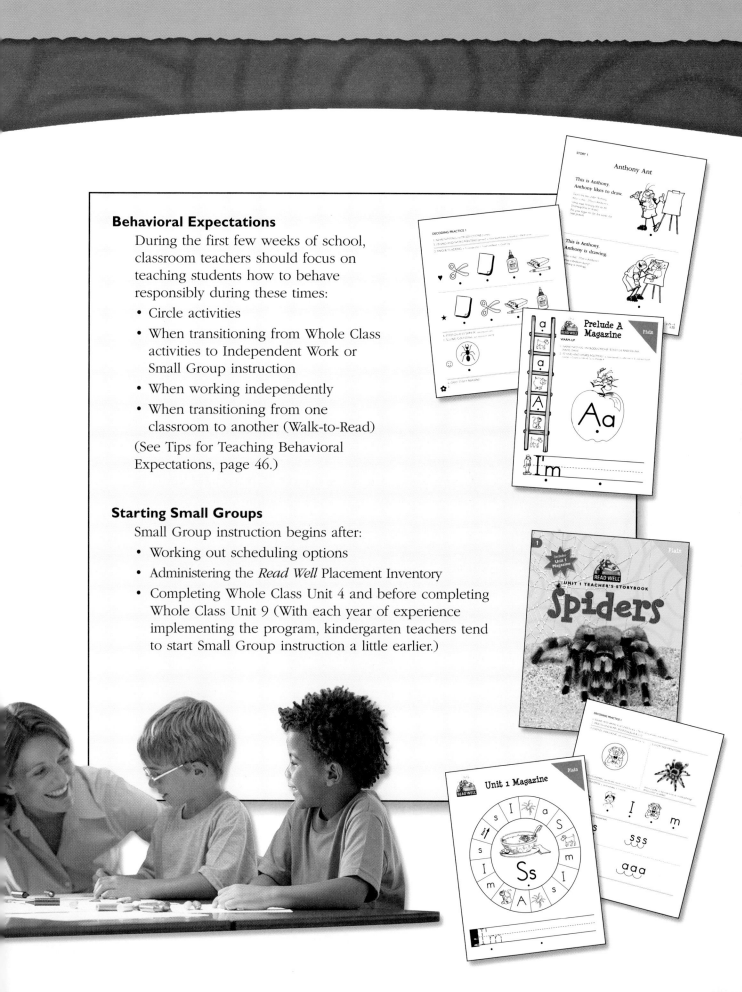

Tips for Teaching Behavioral Expectations

Successful classroom management is a vital part of skilled teaching. In this section, you will learn a few tips for teaching behavioral expectations. TEAM is an adaptation of *CHAMPs* (Sprick, Garrison, & Howard, 1998) for young children. Read *CHAMPs* to gain more in-depth information about managing a classroom.

Identifying Expectations With TEAM

Different settings, activities, and teachers all require young children to engage in varied sets of behaviors. Though some children have the background and ability to intuitively understand what is expected of them, many children need our instruction and ongoing support.

You may wish to use the Talk, Effort, Ask, Move (TEAM) model. TEAM can be used to formulate your behavioral expectations of children during various activities.

Talk	How and when children may talk
Effort	How children should demonstrate effort
Ask	How children can ask for help
Move	How children can move about during an activity

Before the school year starts, develop your own expectations for important activities. Expectations will be used to communicate your vision of what each activity should look and sound like. If you are a classroom teacher, develop expectations for:

- Circle activities
- Transitioning from Whole Class activities to Independent Work or Small Group instruction
- Working independently (see page 48)
- Transitioning from one classroom to another (Walk-to-Read)

Samples of TEAM Expectations

Circle Activities

Expectations for circle activities should reflect the tone you wish to set for Whole Class activities.

Talk	Respond with the group or when called on by the teacher.
Effort	Participate by listening, watching, thinking, nodding, smiling at others, singing, and talking, when appropriate.
Ask	Ask questions and make comments only about what we are talking about.
Move	Sit with your hands and feet to yourself. Stay in our circle.

Transitioning from Whole Class to Independent Work/Small Groups

Develop procedures for moving efficiently from Whole Class activities to Independent Work and, if needed, from Independent Work to Small Group instruction.

Talk	Talk quietly only after you get to your desk or reading group.
Effort	Do your best to stay focused on where *you* need to go.
Ask	Ask questions after you get to your desk or reading group.
Move	Walk quickly to your desk or reading group.

Transitioning From One Class to the Next

If you are implementing a Walk-to-Read schedule, work with your colleagues to develop procedures and expectations for moving from one classroom to the next.

Talk	While waiting in line, talk quietly only to the person next to you.
Effort	Do your best to stay focused on getting to reading class and back on time.
Ask	Ask questions before you leave your classroom or after you get to your reading class.
Move	Line up quickly and quietly at the door. Once in the hall, walk quickly and quietly in a straight line.

Teaching Expectations With TEAM

Across the first few weeks of school, teach and rehearse expectations.

For each activity:

- Explain your expectations using simple rules and visual displays, when appropriate
- Have students role-play expectations
- Provide positive and descriptive feedback
- Have students verify their understanding of expectations

Once expectations have been learned:

- Monitor each activity; provide ongoing, positive, and descriptive feedback
- Periodically, reteach expectations

Samples of TEAM Expectations (*continued*)

Independent Work

Kindergarten is the perfect time for students to learn the important skill of working independently. In the first few weeks of school, begin teaching students to work without your supervision for gradually increasing periods of time. Your expectations should reflect a calm and pleasant classroom.

Talk	Talk quietly in a respectful voice, so that only the person next to you can hear.
Effort	Always do your best to do accurate, complete, and neat work.
Ask	If you need help, ask the person next to you. If you need the teacher's help, walk quietly to the question chair. Remember, only one person may sit in the chair at a time. Take pride in using the chair only when you need help.
Move	Work at your desk. When you are finished working, look at a book from your table's book basket. (*Note:* This expectation will change as students begin learning how to work in centers.)

Explain expectations, using simple rules and visual displays.

I am so pleased to have such a responsible kindergarten class. Everyone in our room is very grown up, or mature, so we're going to practice doing Independent Work. Independent Work is a time when you get to take care of yourself. When you work independently, you can talk quietly, but only to the person next to you. Look at the pocket chart. It shows two students sitting next to each other, working and talking quietly together.

Verify students' understanding.

Everyone, point to the people you can talk to during Independent Work. [Jonathan], who can you talk to during Independent Work? ([Ming and Natalie])

That's right, [Ming] is next to you and so is [Natalie].
[Jonathan], tell [Ming] that she is doing a nice job on her snake book.
Remember to use a voice that only [Ming] and [Natalie] can hear.
Raise your hand if you could hear what Jonathan said.

Have students role-play.

Wow, [Ming] was the only one who could hear what Jonathan said.
[Natalie] couldn't even hear.
[Ming], what did [Jonathan] say? (He said I was doing a nice job.)
Excellent. [Jonathan], you can talk in a grown-up, or mature, working voice.

Provide positive descriptive feedback.

I am very proud of you.
Who else can talk so that only the person next to them can hear?

For each expectation: 1) explain with a simple rule and visual display, 2) verify students' understanding, 3) role-play, and 4) provide postitive descriptive feedback. Have students practice doing Independent Work with you before they are required to do so without supervision.

If your schedule requires group rotations, once Small Group instruction begins, periodically scan independent workers and provide attention to those who are meeting expectations. Effective teachers provide attention before misbehavior occurs from lack of attention.

Teaching Whole Class

This section provides general teaching information and procedures for *Read Well K* Whole Class activities. You will learn how to make use of *Read Well's* teacher-friendly planning features so you can efficiently read, think, and plan!

This section also provides information about how to teach the Alphabet Routines, Read Alouds and Related Activities, and Independent Work.

Read, imagine, practice, and then teach well!

In this section:

Navigating a Unit

Objectives

Each unit opens with a list of the objectives taught and cumulatively reviewed in the unit.

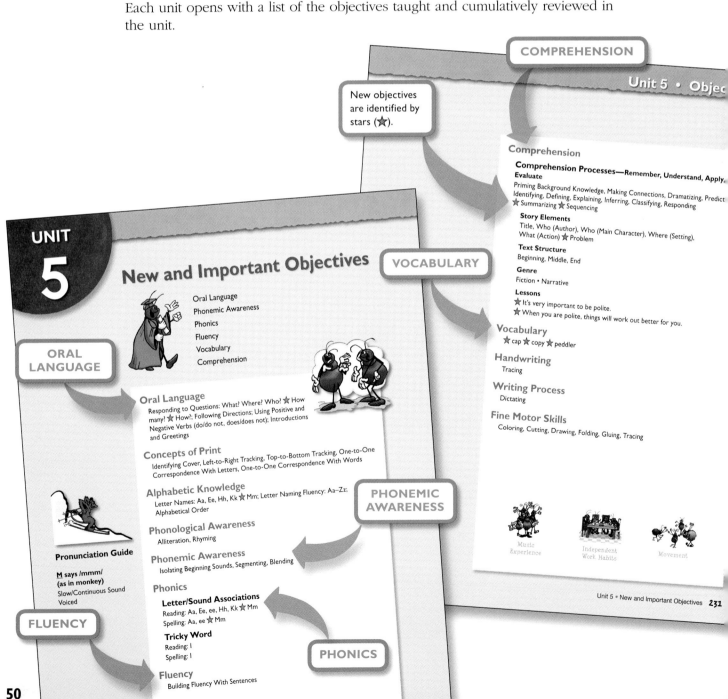

COMPREHENSION

Unit 5 • Obje

New objectives are identified by stars (★).

Comprehension

Comprehension Processes—Remember, Understand, Apply,
Evaluate
Priming Background Knowledge, Making Connections, Dramatizing, Predict
Identifying, Defining, Explaining, Inferring, Classifying, Responding
★ Summarizing ★ Sequencing

Story Elements
Title, Who (Author), Who (Main Character), Where (Setting),
What (Action) ★ Problem

Text Structure
Beginning, Middle, End

Genre
Fiction • Narrative

Lessons
★ It's very important to be polite.
★ When you are polite, things will work out better for you.

Vocabulary
★ cap ★ copy ★ peddler

Handwriting
Tracing

Writing Process
Dictating

Fine Motor Skills
Coloring, Cutting, Drawing, Folding, Gluing, Tracing

VOCABULARY

UNIT

5

New and Important Objectives

Oral Language
Phonemic Awareness
Phonics
Fluency
Vocabulary
Comprehension

ORAL
LANGUAGE

Oral Language
Responding to Questions: What? Where? Who? ★ How
many? ★ How?; Following Directions; Using Positive and
Negative Verbs (do/do not, does/does not); Introductions
and Greetings

Concepts of Print
Identifying Cover, Left-to-Right Tracking, Top-to-Bottom Tracking, One-to-One
Correspondence With Letters, One-to-One Correspondence With Words

Alphabetic Knowledge
Letter Names: Aa, Ee, Hh, Kk ★ Mm; Letter Naming Fluency: Aa–Zz;
Alphabetical Order

Phonological Awareness
Alliteration, Rhyming

PHONEMIC
AWARENESS

Phonemic Awareness
Isolating Beginning Sounds, Segmenting, Blending

Pronunciation Guide

M says /mmm/
(as in monkey)
Slow/Continuous Sound
Voiced

Phonics

Letter/Sound Associations
Reading: Aa, Ee, ee, Hh, Kk ★ Mm
Spelling: Aa, ee ★ Mm

Tricky Word
Reading: I
Spelling: I

FLUENCY

PHONICS

Fluency
Building Fluency With Sentences

Music
Experience

Independent
Work Habits

Movement

Unit 5 • New and Important Objectives **231**

Preparation

Each unit also includes a list of preparation notes for activities that require setup. If you have an instructional assistant or parent volunteers, the preparation notes can be used as a quick guide for laying out tasks for your helpers. If you have an experienced instructional assistant, he or she may use these pages to prepare unit materials well in advance of instruction.

WORK SAMPLES
Samples serve as a powerful inspiration for children to be creative.

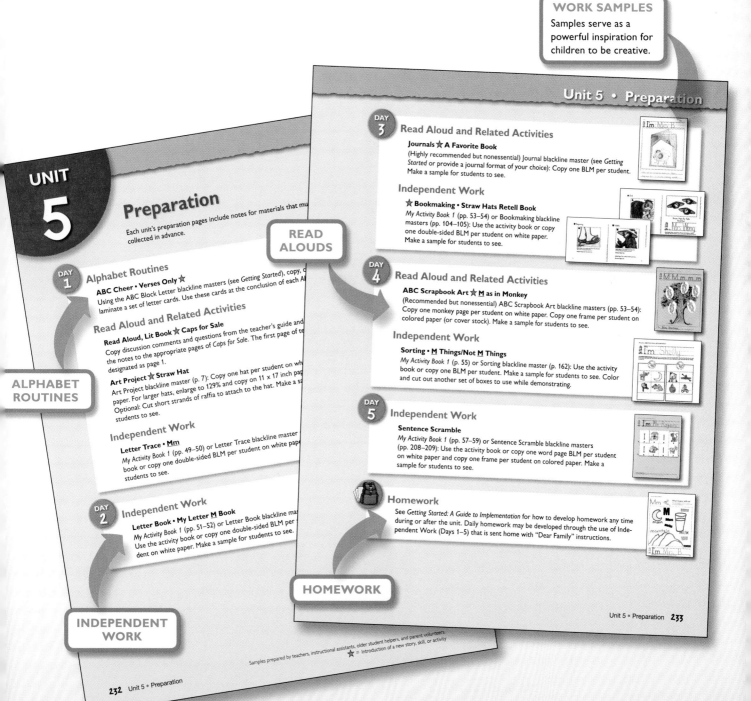

UNIT 5

Preparation

Each unit's preparation pages include notes for materials that mu[...] collected in advance.

ALPHABET ROUTINES

READ ALOUDS

INDEPENDENT WORK

HOMEWORK

DAY 1 Alphabet Routines

ABC Cheer • Verses Only ☆
Using the ABC Block Letter blackline masters (see *Getting Started*), copy, c[...] laminate a set of letter cards. Use these cards at the conclusion of each A[...]

Read Aloud and Related Activities

Read Aloud, Lit Book ☆ Caps for Sale
Copy discussion comments and questions from the teacher's guide and [...] the notes to the appropriate pages of *Caps for Sale*. The first page of te[...] designated as page 1.

Art Project ☆ Straw Hat
Art Project blackline master (p. 7): Copy one hat per student on wh[...] paper. For larger hats, enlarge to 129% and copy on 11 x 17 inch pap[...] Optional: Cut short strands of raffia to attach to the hat. Make a sa[...] students to see.

Independent Work

Letter Trace • Mm
My Activity Book 1 (pp. 49–50) or Letter Trace blackline master [...] book or copy one double-sided BLM per student on white pap[...] students to see.

DAY 2 Independent Work

Letter Book • My Letter M Book
My Activity Book 1 (pp. 51–52) or Letter Book blackline ma[...] Use the activity book or copy one double-sided BLM per [...] dent on white paper. Make a sample for students to see.

DAY 3 Read Aloud and Related Activities

Journals ☆ A Favorite Book
(Highly recommended but nonessential) Journal blackline master (see *Getting Started* or provide a journal format of your choice): Copy one BLM per student. Make a sample for students to see.

Independent Work

☆ Bookmaking • Straw Hats Retell Book
My Activity Book 1 (pp. 53–54) or Bookmaking blackline masters (pp. 104–105): Use the activity book or copy one double-sided BLM per student on white paper. Make a sample for students to see.

DAY 4 Read Aloud and Related Activities

ABC Scrapbook Art ☆ M as in Monkey
(Recommended but nonessential) ABC Scrapbook Art blackline masters (pp. 53–54): Copy one monkey page per student on white paper. Copy one frame per student on colored paper (or cover stock). Make a sample for students to see.

Independent Work

Sorting • M Things/Not M Things
My Activity Book 1 (p. 55) or Sorting blackline master (p. 162): Use the activity book or copy one BLM per student. Make a sample for students to see. Color and cut out another set of boxes to use while demonstrating.

DAY 5 Independent Work

Sentence Scramble
My Activity Book 1 (pp. 57–59) or Sentence Scramble blackline masters (pp. 208–209): Use the activity book or copy one word page BLM per student on white paper and copy one frame per student on colored paper. Make a sample for students to see.

Homework

See *Getting Started: A Guide to Implementation* for how to develop homework any time during or after the unit. Daily homework may be developed through the use of Independent Work (Days 1–5) that is sent home with "Dear Family" instructions.

Samples prepared by teachers, instructional assistants, older student helpers, and parent volunteers.
☆ = Introduction of a new story, skill, or activity

Daily Planner

Following the Preparation pages, each unit includes a Daily Planner. Unit activities are listed for each day, grouped into activity types, and include estimated times and objectives.

UNIT 5

Monkey Business

Slow Letter

M

M says
/mmm/
Continuous
Voiced

Day 1

Alphabet Routines

2 Minutes
Song • Boogie Woogie ABCs (p. 237)
Concepts of Print, Alphabetic Knowledge, Music Experience

4 Minutes
ABC Cheer ☆ New Sound Game ☆ M (p. 237)
ABC Cheer • Verses Only ☆ (p. 239)
Oral Language, Concepts of Print, Alphabetic Knowledge, Phonological Awareness, Phonemic Awareness, Phonics, Music Experience

2 Minutes
Poems ☆ Slow Letter M Review Quick Letter K (p. 240)
Oral Language, Alphabetic Knowledge, Phonological Awareness, Phonemic Awareness, Phonics

2 Minutes
Handwriting • Air and Table Trace ☆ Mm (p. 241)
Concepts of Print, Alphabetic Knowledge, Phonics, Handwriting

Read Alouds and Related Activities

10–15 Minutes
Read Aloud • Lit Book (p. 242)
☆ Caps for Sale
Comprehension, Vocabulary

20 Minutes
Art Project ☆ Straw Hat (p. 245)
Oral Language, Comprehension, Vocabulary, Fine Motor Skills

10 Minutes
Song ☆ Move When It Rhymes (p. 246)
Phonological Awareness, Comprehension, Music Experience, Movement

5 Minutes
Stretch and Shrink ☆ (p. 247)
Oral Language, Phonemic Awareness

Independent Work

15 Minutes
Letter Trace • Mm (p. 249)
Oral Language, Alphabetic Knowledge, Phonics, Handwriting, Fine Motor Skills, Independent Work Habits

Day 2

2 Minutes
ABC Recitation • Alphabet Beat ☆ (p. 251)
Concepts of Print, Alphabetic Knowledge, Music Experience

2 Minutes
ABC Cheer • Verses Only (p. 251)
Alphabetic Knowledge, Phonological Awareness, Phonemic Awareness, Phonics, Music Experience

2 Minutes
Poems • Slow Letter M Review Slow Letter A (p. 252)
Oral Language, Alphabetic Knowledge, Phonological Awareness, Phonemic Awareness, Phonics

2 Minutes
Handwriting • Air and Table Trace Mm (p. 252)
Concepts of Print, Alphabetic Knowledge, Phonics, Handwriting

15–20 Minutes
White Board • Dictate, Copy, and Draw (p. 253)
Oral Language, Concepts of Print, Phonemic Awareness, Phonics, Handwriting, Fine Motor Skills

10–15 Minutes
Read Aloud • Lap Book (p. 254)
☆ Straw Hats for Sale (Chapter 1)
Comprehension, Vocabulary

10 Minutes
Game ☆ Mouse, Mouse, House (p. 255)
Oral Language, Phonological Awareness, Comprehension, Movement

5 Minutes
Smooth and Bumpy Blending (p. 256)
Concepts of Print, Phonemic Awareness, Phonics

15 Minutes
Letter Book • My Letter M Book (p. 257)
Oral Language, Concepts of Print, Alphabetic Knowledge, Phonemic Awareness, Phonics, Handwriting, Fine Motor Skills, Independent Work Habits

☆ = Introduction of a new story, skill, or activity   **RED** titles indicate highly recommended but nonessential activities.

Day 3

2 MINUTES

ABC Recitation • Alphabet Beat (p. 259)
Concepts of Print, Alphabetic Knowledge, Music Experience

2 MINUTES

ABC Cheer • Verses Only (p. 259)
Alphabetic Knowledge, Phonological Awareness, Phonemic Awareness, Phonics, Music Experience

2 MINUTES

**Poems • Slow Letter M
Review Quick Letter K** (p. 260)
Oral Language, Alphabetic Knowledge, Phonological Awareness, Phonemic Awareness, Phonics

Handwriting ☆
Mm (p. 260)
Concepts of Print, Alphabetic Knowledge, Phonics, Handwriting

10–15 MINUTES

Read Aloud • Lap Book (p. 261)
Straw Hats for Sale (☆ Chapter 2)
Comprehension, Vocabulary

20 MINUTES

Journals ☆ **A Favorite Book** (p. 262)
Comprehension, Writing Process, Fine Motor Skills

10 MINUTES

Song • Move When It Rhymes (p. 264)
Phonological Awareness, Comprehension, Music Experience, Movement

10 MINUTES

☆ **Pocket Chart Retell • Straw Hats for Sale** (p. 265)
Comprehension, Vocabulary

15 MINUTES

Bookmaking ☆ **Straw Hats Retell Book** (p. 268)
Oral Language, Comprehension, Fine Motor Skills, Independent Work Habits

Day 4

2 MINUTES

Song • Boogie Woogie ABCs (p. 270)
Concepts of Print, Alphabetic Knowledge, Music Experience

2 MINUTES

ABC Cheer • Verses Only (p. 270)
Alphabetic Knowledge, Phonological Awareness, Phonemic Awareness, Phonics, Music Experience

2 MINUTES

**Poems • Slow Letter M
Review Slow Letter E** (p. 271)
Oral Language, Alphabetic Knowledge, Phonological Awareness, Phonemic Awareness, Phonics

Concepts of Print, Alphabetic Knowledge, Phonics, Handwriting

10–15 MINUTES

Read Aloud • Lit Book Review (p. 272)
Caps for Sale
Comprehension, Vocabulary

20 MINUTES

ABC Scrapbook Art ☆ **M as in Monkey** (p. 274)
Oral Language, Alphabetic Knowledge, Phonemic Awareness, Phonics, Fine Motor Skills

10 MINUTES

Song Review • Variations ☆ (p. 275)
Phonological Awareness, Music Experience, Movement

5 MINUTES

Stretch and Shrink (p. 276)
Oral Language, Phonemic Awareness

15–20 MINUTES

Sorting ☆ **M Things/Not M Things** (p. 277)
Oral Language, Comprehension, Phonics, Fine Motor Skills, Independent Work Habits

Day 5

2 MINUTES

ABC Recitation • Alphabet Beat (p. 279)
Concepts of Print, Alphabetic Knowledge, Music Experience

2 MINUTES

ABC Cheer • Verses Only (p. 279)
Alphabetic Knowledge, Phonological Awareness

2 MINUTES

**Poems • Slow Letter M
Review Quick Letter K** (p. 280)
Oral Language, Alphabetic Knowledge, Phonological Awareness, Phonemic Awareness, Phonics

Concepts of Print, Alphabetic Knowledge, Phonics, Handwriting

15–20 MINUTES

White Board • Dictate, Copy, and Draw ☆ (p. 281)
Oral Language, Concepts of Print, Phonemic Awareness, Phonics, Handwriting, Fine Motor Skills

10–15 MINUTES

Read Aloud • Teacher's Choice

5 MINUTES

Smooth and Bumpy Blending ☆ (p. 284)
Concepts of Print, Phonemic Awareness, Phonics

10 MINUTES

Pocket Chart ☆ **Sentence Building** (p. 285)
Concepts of Print, Phonics, Fluency, Vocabulary

15 MINUTES

Sentence Scramble (p. 287)
Oral Language, Concepts of Print, Phonics, Fluency, Fine Motor Skills, Independent Work Habits

BLACK titles indicate essential activities

RED titles indicate highly recommended but nonessential activities

Stars (☆) = Introduction of a new story, skill, or activity

At a Glance

At a Glance provides an easy-to-read outline of a day's activities.

Alphabet Routines

The Alphabet Routines can be done as shown, or divided across your day.

Read Aloud and Related Activities

The Read Aloud and Related Activities may be scheduled across six days if needed.

Activities can be done in any sequence, with the following exceptions:

- Day 3 Read Aloud must precede Day 3 Pocket Chart Activity.
- Day 3 Pocket Chart Activity must precede Day 3 Independent Work.
- Day 5 Pocket Chart Activity must precede Day 5 Independent Work.

Independent Work

If Small Groups are taught concurrently, Independent Work is not needed. *Read Well K* Independent Work for Days 1, 2, and 4 can be used as an activity for students to work on as they start their day.

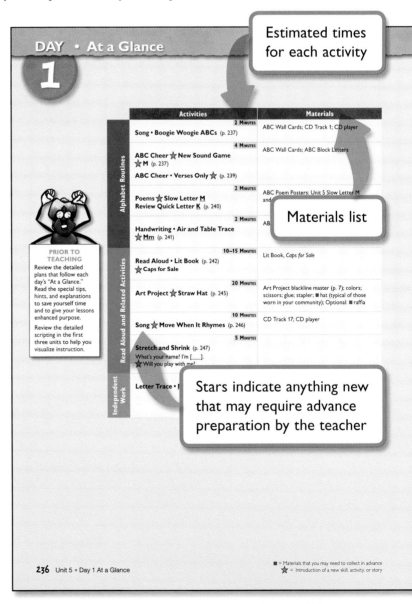

Principles of Whole Class Instruction

The Important Role of the Teacher

Just as an accomplished musician deserves an excellent instrument, teachers deserve excellent programs. *Read Well K* is a finely tuned instrument, but it requires dedicated professionals to implement it with skill, joy, and sensitivity. You are critical to the children's success.

Systematic and Explicit Instruction

Explicit teaching gently scaffolds teacher support. When a new skill is introduced, teachers overtly demonstrate or model. Next, teachers guide or practice with the children. Finally, teachers encourage children to do it "all by yourselves." (The scaffolding is removed.)

When lessons are focused on specific skills, you will:

- **Demonstrate**
- **Guide practice**
- **Mix group and individual turns, independent of your voice**

Note: By its heterogeneous nature, Whole Class instruction is not mastery based.

Scripting

HOW TO DELIVER THE PROGRAM

Whole Class activities are scripted for the purpose of helping you visualize instruction before you teach. The scripts give you the important steps in the lesson, but they are not intended to be memorized or read aloud to students.

In the early units, take the time to study the scripts. Imagine yourself working with children. Talk yourself through the lessons. As you gradually internalize the critical steps of instruction, you will find yourself using *Read Well* with skill and confidence.

As you move through the program, the scripts will:

- Provide assistance to substitutes and to teachers hired midyear
- Provide you with a refresher, when needed
- Introduce new activities
- Help you maximize opportunities to learn

Teacher talk:
Blue text

Student responses with the teacher:
Gray text

Student responses without the teacher:
(Gray text in parentheses)

Word choices that can be tailored to the group (names, objects, phrases):
[Bracketed text]

Letters that are referred to by name are underlined: e

Smooth and Bumpy Blending

5 Minutes

Students practice Smooth and Bumpy Blending of the letter a and the letter e and continue discrimination practice as they choose whether to do Smooth Blending or Bumpy Blending. Students are introduced to Smooth Blending of the rhyming words: me, see, and we.

★❶ Introduce Blending Card 16. Demonstrate and guide Smooth Blending the words: me, see, we.

- Demonstrate Smooth Blending: /mmmēēē/.
  I'm going to do Smooth Blending.
  Loop under each letter. /mmmēēē/
  The word is me.
  Look at me.

- Guide Smooth Blending: /mmmēēē/.
  Let's do Smooth Blending together.
  Loop under each sound. /mmmēēē/
  Say the word. (me)

- Repeat with group and individual turns, independent of your voice.
  - Repeat with: /sssēēē/.
  ◆◆ What do you see? (I see [books].)

  - Repeat with: /wwwēēē/.
  ◆◆ What are we doing? (We are [reading].)

- Identify the rhyming words.
  You just read the words me, see, and we.
  These words rhyme. They all end with /ēēē/.

- Have students identify the rhyming words.
  Point to "me." Say the word. (me)
  Point to "see." Say the word. (see)
  Point to "we." Say the word. (we)
  These words all end with /ēēē/. These words rhyme.

me

see

we

How to Teach the Alphabet Routines

The Alphabet Routines include the ABC Poems and quick, jazzy little songs and verses your students will grow to love. Study the scripts. Listen to the CD. Before you know it, you and your children will be singing, tapping, and jamming together. The daily repetition is vital to building fluency and deep letter/sound knowledge.

What's Included

- **Boogie Woogie ABCs**
  (CD, ABC Wall Cards)

- **ABC Cheer**
  New Sound Intro (ABC Wall Cards, CD with Units 1–4)

- **ABC Cheer**
  Verses Only and Full Cheer
  (ABC Wall Cards, CD with Units 1–4, 9, 18, 26)

- **ABC Poems**
  (ABC Poem Posters)

- **Handwriting, Air and Table Trace**
  (CD, ABC Wall Cards)

- **Alphabet Beat**
  (CD, ABC Wall Cards)

- **Zee-Zi-Ziddly**
  (CD, ABC Wall Cards)

Sound Pronunciations

Read Well K introduces sound pronunciations that have been selected for their linguistic accuracy and ease of letter/sound blending.

Because teachers have learned different sound pronunciations, it is important to check out your own pronunciations and to practice. Listen to the *Alphabet Cheer* on the *Read Well K* CD. (Students learn one new letter/sound association at a time. Preview the entire sequence of sounds by listening to CD Track 38 while following the Sound Pronunciation chart.)

Sound Pronunciations (continued)

HOW TO PRACTICE LETTER/SOUND ASSOCIATIONS

CONTINUOUS SOUNDS can be pronounced as long as you have the breath to say them. Continuous (slow) sounds are shown by three repeating letters in slashes (/ăăă/).

QUICK SOUNDS are co-articulated with the adjoining vowels in words. In isolated sound practice, quick sounds must be pronounced briefly (/b/ not /bŭh/, /g/ not /gŭh/). Quick sounds are shown by an individual letter in slashes (/k/).

ARTICULATION
Accept close approximations when working with English Language Learners and children who have articulation problems. Work closely with speech and language specialists.

Aa /ăăă/ **Ant** Continuous Voiced (Short) **Unit 1**	**Ee** /ēēē/ **Eel** Continuous Voiced (Long) **Unit 2**	**Hh** /h/ **Horse** Quick Unvoiced (not huh) **Unit 3**	**Kk** /k/ **Kayak** Quick Unvoiced (not kuh) **Unit 4**	**Mm** /mmm/ **Monkey** Continuous Voiced **Unit 5**
Rr /rrr/ **Rooster** Continuous Voiced **Unit 6**	**Ss** /sss/ **Spider** Continuous Unvoiced **Unit 7**	**Ww** /www/ **Worm** Continuous Voiced (woo) **Unit 8**	**Zz** /zzz/ **Zebra** Continuous Voiced **Unit 9**	**Cc** /k/ **Cow** Quick Unvoiced (not kuh) **Unit 10**
Dd /d/ **Dog** Quick Voiced (not duh) **Unit 11**	**Ii** /ĭĭĭ/ **Insect** Continuous Voiced (Short) **Unit 12**	**Jj** /j/ **Jellybean** Quick Voiced (not juh) **Unit 13**	**Nn** /nnn/ **Nurse** Continuous Voiced **Unit 14**	**Pp** /p/ **Policeman** Quick Unvoiced (not puh) **Unit 15**
Tt /t/ **Turtle** Quick Unvoiced (not tuh) **Unit 16**	**Vv** /vvv/ **Violin** Continuous Voiced **Unit 17**	**Yy** /y-/ **Yak** Quick Voiced **Unit 18**	**Ee** /ĕĕĕ/ **Ed or Engine** Continuous Voiced (Short) **Short Vowel E**	**Bb** /b/ **Bee** Quick Voiced (not buh) **Unit 19**
Ff /fff/ **Flower** Continuous Unvoiced **Unit 20**	**Gg** /g/ **Goose** Quick Voiced (not guh) **Unit 21**	**Ll** /lll/ **Lobster** Continuous Voiced **Unit 22**	**Oo** /ŏŏŏ/ **Octopus** Continuous Voiced (Short) **Unit 23**	**Qu/qu** /kw/ **Quail** Quick Unvoiced **Unit 24**
Uu /ŭŭŭ/ **Umbrella** Continuous Voiced (Short) **Unit 25**	**Xx** /ksss/ **X-ray** Continuous Unvoiced **Unit 26**			

Boogie Woogie ABCs

Getting to Know the Boogie Woogie ABCs

Step 1. Listen to the *Boogie Woogie ABCs* on Track 1 of the *Read Well K* CD of Songs.

Step 2. Skim the directions for the Day 1 introduction of the *Boogie Woogie ABCs*.

Step 3. Read the text below. The boxed notes clarify the importance of the notations in the teacher's guides.

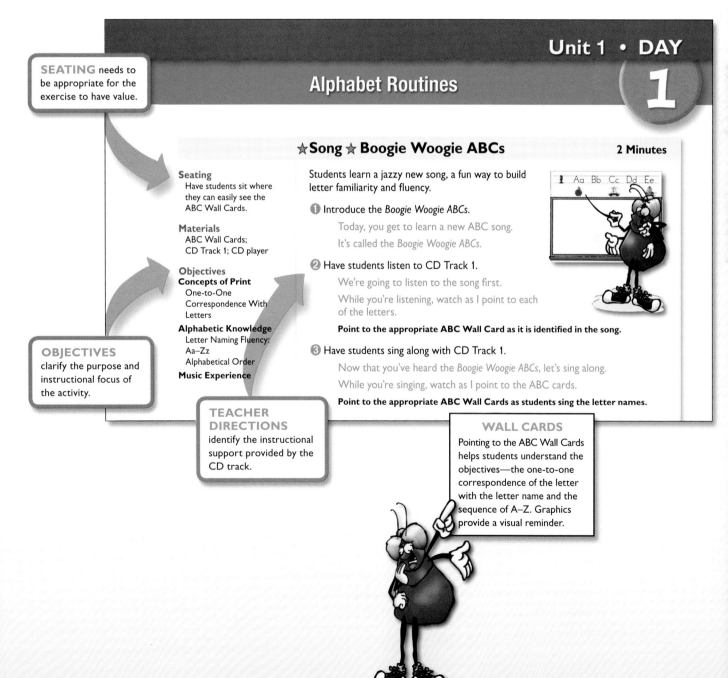

SEATING needs to be appropriate for the exercise to have value.

OBJECTIVES clarify the purpose and instructional focus of the activity.

TEACHER DIRECTIONS identify the instructional support provided by the CD track.

WALL CARDS
Pointing to the ABC Wall Cards helps students understand the objectives—the one-to-one correspondence of the letter with the letter name and the sequence of A–Z. Graphics provide a visual reminder.

Unit 1 • DAY 1

Alphabet Routines

☆Song ☆ Boogie Woogie ABCs — 2 Minutes

Students learn a jazzy new song, a fun way to build letter familiarity and fluency.

❶ Introduce the *Boogie Woogie ABCs*.

> Today, you get to learn a new ABC song.
>
> It's called the *Boogie Woogie ABCs*.

❷ Have students listen to CD Track 1.

> We're going to listen to the song first.
>
> While you're listening, watch as I point to each of the letters.

Point to the appropriate ABC Wall Card as it is identified in the song.

❸ Have students sing along with CD Track 1.

> Now that you've heard the *Boogie Woogie ABCs*, let's sing along.
>
> While you're singing, watch as I point to the ABC cards.

Point to the appropriate ABC Wall Cards as students sing the letter names.

Seating
Have students sit where they can easily see the ABC Wall Cards.

Materials
ABC Wall Cards; CD Track 1; CD player

Objectives
Concepts of Print
One-to-One Correspondence With Letters

Alphabetic Knowledge
Letter Naming Fluency: Aa–Zz
Alphabetical Order

Music Experience

ABC Cheer, New Sound Intro, and New Sound Game

Getting to Know the Cheer and Intro

Step 1. Skim the directions for the Unit 4, Day 1 *ABC Cheer* and New Sound Intro.

Step 2. Listen to CD Track 13 on the *Read Well K CD of Songs*.

Step 3. Read the text below. The boxed notes clarify the importance of the notations in the teacher's guides.

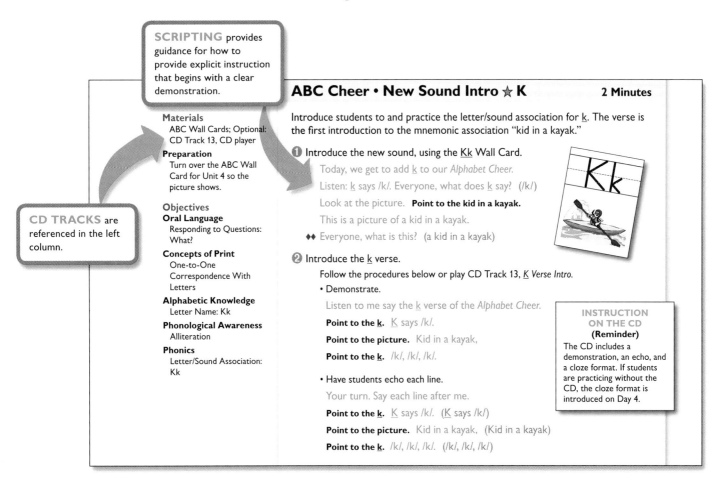

SCRIPTING provides guidance for how to provide explicit instruction that begins with a clear demonstration.

CD TRACKS are referenced in the left column.

Materials
ABC Wall Cards; Optional: CD Track 13, CD player

Preparation
Turn over the ABC Wall Card for Unit 4 so the picture shows.

Objectives
Oral Language
Responding to Questions: What?

Concepts of Print
One-to-One Correspondence With Letters

Alphabetic Knowledge
Letter Name: Kk

Phonological Awareness
Alliteration

Phonics
Letter/Sound Association: Kk

ABC Cheer • New Sound Intro ☆ K   2 Minutes

Introduce students to and practice the letter/sound association for k. The verse is the first introduction to the mnemonic association "kid in a kayak."

1 Introduce the new sound, using the Kk Wall Card.

Today, we get to add k to our *Alphabet Cheer.*

Listen: k says /k/. Everyone, what does k say? (/k/)

Look at the picture. **Point to the kid in a kayak.**

This is a picture of a kid in a kayak.

◆◆ Everyone, what is this? (a kid in a kayak)

2 Introduce the k verse.

Follow the procedures below or play CD Track 13, *K Verse Intro.*

• Demonstrate.

Listen to me say the k verse of the *Alphabet Cheer.*

Point to the k. K says /k/.

Point to the picture. Kid in a kayak,

Point to the k. /k/, /k/, /k/.

• Have students echo each line.

Your turn. Say each line after me.

Point to the k. K says /k/. (K says /k/)

Point to the picture. Kid in a kayak, (Kid in a kayak)

Point to the k. /k/, /k/, /k/. (/k/, /k/, /k/)

INSTRUCTION ON THE CD (Reminder)
The CD includes a demonstration, an echo, and a cloze format. If students are practicing without the CD, the cloze format is introduced on Day 4.

New Sound Game

In Units 5–26, the teacher introduces the new sound, then students guess what pictures might be on the new ABC Wall Card. Ham it up to create anticipation! Don't let anyone peek at the pictures.

As you turn over each new card, your students will clap with delight. "Oh, it's a monkey on a mountain." As students guess what might be pictured on the ABC Wall Card, they develop phonemic awareness skills and have fun at the same time.

Getting to Know the Verses Only

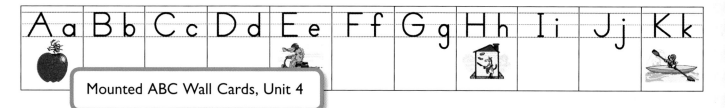

Mounted ABC Wall Cards, Unit 4

To maintain instructional focus, do not display or turn over key word pictures until the letter/sound association is introduced. This purposeful introduction makes learning manageable for students who enter kindergarten with limited letter/sound knowledge.

Step 1. Skim the directions for the Unit 4, Day 1 *ABC Cheer* • Verses Only section.

Step 2. Listen to CD Track 14 on the *Read Well K* CD of Songs.

Step 3. Read the text below. The boxed notes clarify the significance of the color-coded script and highlight other important instructional features.

GUIDE students with your voice when gray student responses are not in parentheses. This is cued by the script "Let's say the verses . . ."

MRS. B'S NOTES provide important instructional tips. The scaffolding note encourages you to begin fading your voice on known verses. This step encourages children to develop confidence and independence.

SCAFFOLDING (Reminder)
Encourage independent responses. Start the *Alphabet Cheer* with your voice, then fade your voice out on the known verses. Continue guiding the new <u>k</u> verse, as needed.

ABC Cheer • Verses Only — 2 Minutes

Cards; Optional: 14, CD player

Knowledge
Letter Names: Aa, Ee, Hh, Kk

cal Awareness
Awareness
eginning Sounds

und Associations:
n, Kk

erience

The *Alphabet Cheer* provides daily practice with the new letter/sound association and an important cumulative review of all previously learned sounds. The random review of beginning sounds at the conclusion of the *Alphabet Cheer* provides practice in discriminating beginning sounds outside of the familiar sequence of the cheer.

❶ Have students practice the *Alphabet Cheer*—saying known verses only.

Follow the procedures below or play CD Track 14, *Alphabet Cheer, Units 1–4.*

Say the verses with students, only as needed.

Let's say the verses of the *Alphabet Cheer* that we've learned so far.

Point to the <u>a</u>. A says /ăăă/.
Point to the picture. Ant on an apple,
Point to the <u>a</u>. /ă/, /ă/, /ăăă/.

Point to the <u>e</u>. E says /ēēē/.
Point to the picture. Eel on wheels,
Point to the <u>e</u>. /ē/, /ē/, /ēēē/.

Point to the <u>h</u>. H says /h/.
Point to the picture. Horse in a house,
Point to the <u>h</u>. /h/, /h/, /h/.

Point to the <u>k</u>. K says /k/.
Point to the picture. Kid in a kayak,
Point to the <u>k</u>. /k/, /k/, k/.

CRITICAL STEPS are included in instruction. Practicing the sounds out of order prevents students from depending on the sequence of the verses for letter recognition.

❷ Have students review beginning sounds in random order.
Point to the eel. What sound do you hear at the beginning of *eel*? (/ēēē/)
Point to the kayak. What sound do you hear at the beginning of *kayak*? (/k/)
Point to the ant. What sound do you hear at the beginning of *ant*? (/ăăă/)
Point to the horse. What sound do you hear at the beginning of *horse*? (/h/)

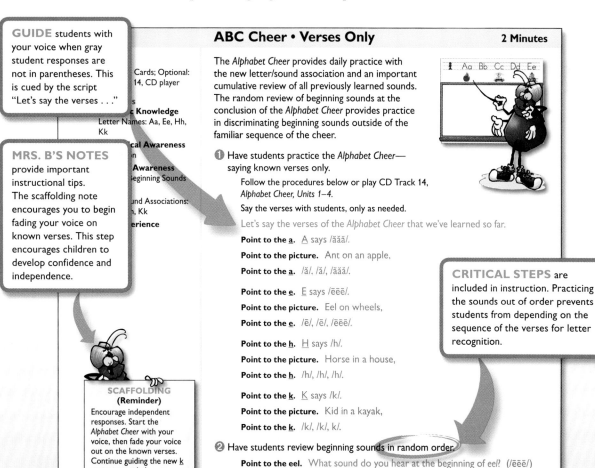

ABC Cheer • Full Cheer

Getting to Know the Full Cheer

Step 1. Skim the directions for the Unit 9, Day 1 *ABC Cheer* • Full Cheer section.

Step 2. Listen to CD Track 20 on the *Read Well K* CD of Songs while following the ABC Wall Cards.

Step 3. Practice with Track 20. For this unit, pictures would be turned over for A, E, H, K, M, R, S, W, and Z.

❸ Have students say the full *Alphabet Cheer* along with CD Track 20.
Guide students, only as needed.

A says /ăăă/. Ant on an apple, /ă/, /ă/, /ăăă/.

B, C, D,

E says /ēēē/. Eel on wheels, /ē/, /ē/, /ēēē/.

F, G,

H says /h/. Horse in a house, /h/, /h/, /h/.

I,

J,

K says /k/. Kid in a kayak, /k/, /k/, /k/.

L, M says /mmm/. Monkey on a mountain, /m/, /m/, /mmm/.

N, O, P, Q,

R says /rrr/. Rooster on the roof, /r/, /r/, /rrr/.

S says /sss/. Spider in the soup, /s/, /s/, /sss/.

T, U, V,

W says /www/. Worm in a wagon, /w/, /w/, /www/.

X, Y,

Z says /zzz/. Zebra in the zoo, /z/, /z/, /zzz/.

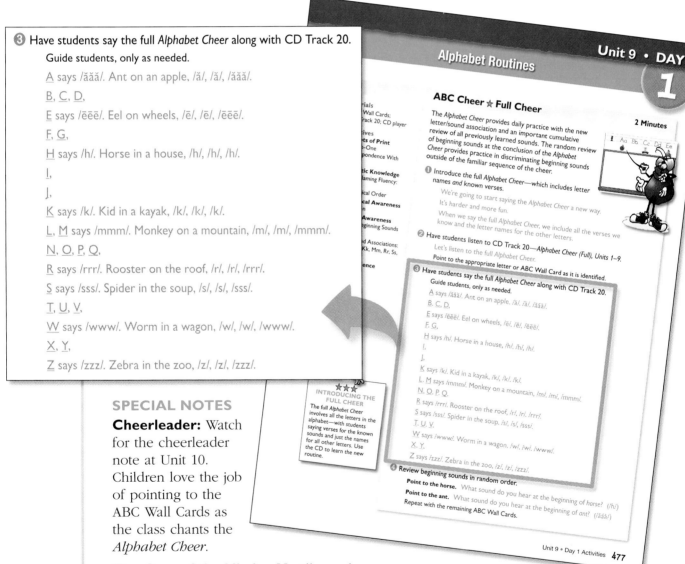

SPECIAL NOTES

Cheerleader: Watch for the cheerleader note at Unit 10. Children love the job of pointing to the ABC Wall Cards as the class chants the *Alphabet Cheer*.

The Case of the Missing X: All year long, students wait to turn over the last ABC Wall Card in the alphabet. But when they get to Unit 26, the Xx Wall Card goes missing. It's a class mystery! If your curiosity has been tickled, read Unit 26 to discover what lies ahead for you and your students at the end of the year.

ABC Poem

Getting to Know the ABC Poem

Step 1. Skim the directions for the Unit 8, Day 1 poem.

Step 2. Read the text below. The boxed notes clarify the importance of the notations in the teacher's guides.

Step 3. Practice introducing *Slow Letter* <u>W</u>, following the script in the teacher's guide.

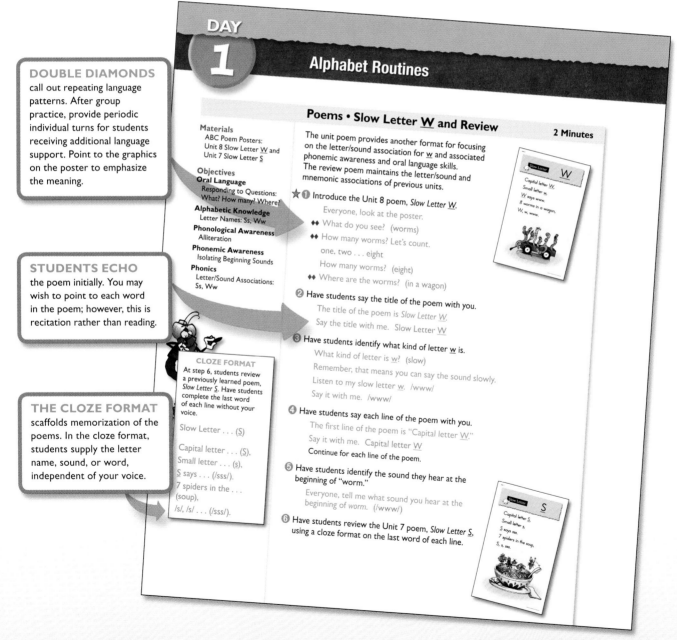

DOUBLE DIAMONDS
call out repeating language patterns. After group practice, provide periodic individual turns for students receiving additional language support. Point to the graphics on the poster to emphasize the meaning.

STUDENTS ECHO
the poem initially. You may wish to point to each word in the poem; however, this is recitation rather than reading.

THE CLOZE FORMAT
scaffolds memorization of the poems. In the cloze format, students supply the letter name, sound, or word, independent of your voice.

DAY 1
Alphabet Routines

Poems • Slow Letter <u>W</u> and Review
2 Minutes

Materials
ABC Poem Posters:
Unit 8 Slow Letter <u>W</u> and
Unit 7 Slow Letter <u>S</u>

Objectives
Oral Language
Responding to Questions:
What? How many? Where?
Alphabetic Knowledge
Letter Names: Ss, Ww
Phonological Awareness
Alliteration
Phonemic Awareness
Isolating Beginning Sounds
Phonics
Letter/Sound Associations:
Ss, Ww

The unit poem provides another format for focusing on the letter/sound association for <u>w</u> and associated phonemic awareness and oral language skills. The review poem maintains the letter/sound and mnemonic associations of previous units.

⭐ ❶ Introduce the Unit 8 poem, *Slow Letter* <u>W</u>.
Everyone, look at the poster.
♦♦ What do you see? (worms)
♦♦ How many worms? Let's count.
one, two . . . eight
How many worms? (eight)
♦♦ Where are the worms? (in a wagon)

❷ Have students say the title of the poem with you.
The title of the poem is *Slow Letter W*.
Say the title with me. *Slow Letter W*

❸ Have students identify what kind of letter <u>w</u> is.
What kind of letter is <u>w</u>? (slow)
Remember, that means you can say the sound slowly.
Listen to my slow letter <u>w</u>. /www/
Say it with me. /www/

❹ Have students say each line of the poem with you.
The first line of the poem is "Capital letter <u>W</u>."
Say it with me. Capital letter <u>W</u>
Continue for each line of the poem.

❺ Have students identify the sound they hear at the beginning of "worm."
Everyone, tell me what sound you hear at the beginning of *worm*. (/www/)

❻ Have students review the Unit 7 poem, *Slow Letter* <u>S</u>, using a cloze format on the last word of each line.

CLOZE FORMAT
At step 6, students review a previously learned poem, *Slow Letter S*. Have students complete the last word of each line without your voice.

Slow Letter . . . (<u>S</u>)

Capital letter . . . (<u>S</u>),
Small letter . . . (<u>s</u>),
<u>S</u> says . . . (/sss/).
7 spiders in the . . . (soup),
/s/, /s/ . . . (/sss/).

Note: When a letter is underlined, say the letter name. When a letter or letters are in slashes, say the sound.

Handwriting • Air and Table Trace

Getting to Know the Tracing Exercise

Because of the young age of the children, *Read Well K* does not emphasize handwriting. However, the program also does not leave children to work out their own system of handwriting. Each day, students do a simple air and table trace—following your model. Independent Work provides guidelines to *help* children feel successful, without requiring perfection.

SPECIAL FEATURE

The Theo Bear icon (named in honor of Dr. Seuss—Theodor Seuss Geisel) provides a reference for the writing lines. The top line is referred to as the *hat line*, the middle line is the *belt line*, and the bottom line is the *shoe line*. Have fun with CD Track 4 as students learn about the guidelines in a new rendition of *If You're Happy and You Know It*.

See the Unit 1, Day 2 facsimile below for a preview of how to teach Handwriting • Air and Table Trace.

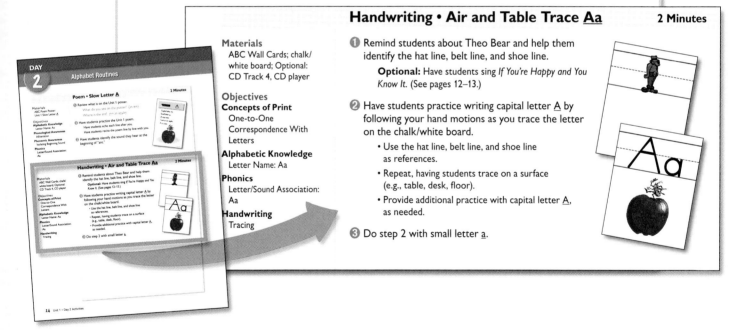

Handwriting • Air and Table Trace Aa   2 Minutes

Materials
ABC Wall Cards; chalk/white board; Optional: CD Track 4, CD player

Objectives
Concepts of Print
One-to-One Correspondence With Letters

Alphabetic Knowledge
Letter Name: Aa

Phonics
Letter/Sound Association: Aa

Handwriting
Tracing

① Remind students about Theo Bear and help them identify the hat line, belt line, and shoe line.

> **Optional:** Have students sing *If You're Happy and You Know It*. (See pages 12–13.)

② Have students practice writing capital letter A by following your hand motions as you trace the letter on the chalk/white board.

- Use the hat line, belt line, and shoe line as references.
- Repeat, having students trace on a surface (e.g., table, desk, floor).
- Provide additional practice with capital letter A, as needed.

③ Do step 2 with small letter a.

Have fun with the Alphabet Routines. Once you've studied the scripts and understand the routines, watch for the ★s. The stars signal when something new is being introduced.

Read. Listen. Imagine. Have fun!

How to Teach Read Alouds and Related Activities

This section is a smorgasbord of activities, rich in content and purpose. Each day, you will read to your children, take them through activities that engage them in a topic, foster curiosity, and build interest in the world around them. While building phonemic awareness, phonics skills, and content knowledge, your children will play with dough, plant seeds, sing, talk, and learn to work and play together.

- **Read Alouds**
  Day 1, Lit Book (26 literature books in all)
  Days 2 and 3, Lap Book (9 Lap Books, 26 units, 2 stories per unit)
  Day 4, Review (recommended but nonessential)
  Day 5, Teacher's Choice
- **Art Projects**
  (Blackline masters; Units 1–8 and 10 required; Unit 9 and others recommended but nonessential)
- **Songs**
  (CD of Songs)
- **ABC Poems**
  (ABC Poem Posters)
- **ABC Scrapbook**
  (Blackline masters; recommended but not required)
- **Journals**
  (Blackline masters located in the appendix of this guide; highly recommended but nonessential)
- **Pocket Chart Activities**
  (Pocket Chart Cards)
- **Games**
  (Blackline masters located in the appendix of this guide)
- **Stretch and Shrink**
- **White Board • Dictate, Copy, and Draw**
- **Smooth and Bumpy Blending**
  (Whole Class Blending Cards)

Lit Book, Day 1

The *Read Well K* Read Aloud stories are a mix of multiple genres, including wonderful works of fiction—ABC books, predictable books, books with rhythm and rhyme, imaginative selections, traditional folktales, and realistic narratives. The program also includes a broad selection of literature books and Lap Book selections that feature expository content. With these books, you will capture the natural curiosity of children as they learn about spiders, worms, plants, the gentle giant octopus, and more.

Getting to Know the Read Aloud

Read Well K Lit Books were carefully selected to match the attention span and interest of young children. Day 1 of each unit opens with a celebrated children's book. Follow the Unit 8 sample provided here to preview the basic procedures.

Step 1. Locate the Lit Book *Wonderful Worms*.

Step 2. Copy the discussion comments and questions from the teacher's guide onto sticky notes. Affix the notes to the appropriate pages of the book. Unless the book has its own page numbers, the first page of text is designated as page 1.

Step 3. Practice reading the story with the discussion questions and comments.

Step 4. Review the objectives listed above each set of questions and comments. The dialogue primes background knowledge and helps students **identify important information**. Students also **build knowledge**, **make connections**, **explain**, **describe**, **infer**, **summarize**, and **respond**.

DAY 1

Read Aloud and Related Activities

Read Aloud • Lit Book

10–15 Minutes

Seating
Have students sit where they can easily see the book.

Materials
Lit Book, *Wonderful Worms*

Preparation
Copy discussion comments and questions and affix the notes to the appropriate pages of *Wonderful Worms*. The first page of text is designated as page 1.

Objectives
Comprehension
Remember
 Identifying
Understand
 Dramatizing,
 Demonstrating,
 Summarizing
Apply
 Priming Background
 Knowledge, Making
 Connections, Explaining,
 Inferring
Evaluate
 Responding
Story Element
 Author
Expository Element
 Facts
Genre
 Nonfiction • Expository
Vocabulary
 Defining and Using: burrow,
 earthworm

Young children have a natural fascination with earthworms. Glaser's book provides interesting facts about these burrowing creatures and how they help plants grow. Children will build background knowledge, learn to identify facts, summarize facts, and apply facts to explain events in nature.

⭐ **Wonderful Worms**
by Linda Glaser
Earthworms are fascinating creatures! They don't have eyes, ears, or a nose, but they use their bodies to burrow in the earth and to feel the vibrations of sounds. This book is full of fun facts that give a glimpse into the unique life of the earthworm.

❶ Introduce the story.

Priming Background Knowledge, Making Connections, Explaining
• Say something like:
 I like to study earthworms.
 Raise your hand if you have ever looked closely at a worm.
 Make a wiggly worm with your fingers.
 Put your hand on your head if you've ever held a worm.
 What did it feel like?
 What did it do?

Identifying—Author
• While showing students the book cover, say:
 The title of our story is *Wonderful Worms*.
 The story was written by Linda Glaser, so Linda Glaser is the . . . (author).
 The person who drew the pictures is Loretta Krupinski.

❷ Read the book out loud to students and discuss the content and pictures by asking questions and making comments as you read. As students respond, think aloud with them. *Note:* You may wish to modify the instruction based on the background knowledge of your students.

Identifying—Where, What
a. After reading page 3, say:
 Point to the picture. Look at the picture.
 Where do worms live? (underground)
 What else do you see living underground? (a mouse)

(continued)

422 Unit 8 • Day 1 Activities

⭐ = Introduction of a new skill, activity, or story

Lit Book, Day 1 (continued)

DAY 1

PARAPHRASING by the teacher provides a demonstration of how to quickly summarize important information.

COMPREHENSION QUESTIONS (Reminder)
The programmed questions and comments help students focus on important comprehension strategies.

VOCABULARY is introduced with a picture or a student-friendly definition.

Then the word is used both meaningfully and frequently.

ACTIVE ENGAGEMENT is guided by the script as students briefly demonstrate things they are hearing about.

RESPONSES to information presented in the text are modeled by the teacher and then followed by opportunities for students to respond.

Unit 8 • DAY 1

Read Aloud and Related Activities

Read Aloud (continued)

Inferring

b. After reading page 5, say:

Earthworms feel sounds with their whole bodies.

What do you think the earthworm in this picture can feel? ([the boy walking])

Identifying—Where; Defining Vocabulary—burrow

c. After reading page 6, say:

Look at the picture. Who can show me where the earthworm lives?

That's called a *burrow*.

Identifying; Using Vocabulary—burrow; Inferring; Explaining

d. On page 7, say:

Look at the picture.

Does an earthworm use a shovel to dig its burrow? (no)

How do you think it makes its burrow?

Identifying—Fact; Explaining

e. After reading page 9, say:

How do worms dig passageways and burrows? (by eating)

We just learned an interesting fact.

Earthworms dig their burrows by eating dirt.

Help me tell that fact. Earthworms dig their burrows by . . . (eating dirt).

Explaining, Demonstrating

f. After reading page 11, say:

How does an earthworm move? (It stretches and squeezes.)

Demonstrate stretching and squeezing your hand.

Look at my hand. Pretend it's an earthworm.

First it stretches out. Then it squeezes in.

Stretch and squeeze, stretch and squeeze. You try it.

Identifying—What

g. After reading page 13, say:

Look at this picture. What do you see?

Responding

h. After reading page 15, say:

So earthworms help the plants breathe and grow.

I think that makes earthworms very important.

What do you think?

(continued)

Lap Book, Days 2 and 3

In the Lap Book Read Alouds, students engage in prediction, dramatic play, sing alongs, and summarization of facts and narratives. Because of the interactive nature of the lessons, it is important to preview each selection before reading it to your class.

Getting to Know a Nonfiction Selection

Step 1. Turn to page 32 in Lap Book 3, *Spiders, Worms, and Bugs, Oh My!* The Preparation tip lets you know what is needed for the lesson. In Unit 8, you will need a partially filled water balloon to demonstrate the vocabulary word "vibration."

Step 2. Read the Introduction. In each story, you will read the small gray text to students. The Introduction primes background knowledge, reviews a previous chapter, introduces new vocabulary, and/or encourages students to make predictions.

Step 3. Read the Lap Book selection. At the conclusion, note how this nonfiction selection ends with a fact summary.

Step 4. Review the vocabulary building dialogue on page 35 of Lap Book 3.

Earthworms don't have ears, but their body has special parts to help them feel things move. If you were an earthworm, you would feel *vibrations* in the ground.

Vibrations. That's a great word. Everyone say *vibrations.* (vibrations)
I've made a water balloon.
When I hold the water balloon in the palm of my hand and give it a firm tap, it vibrates, or moves.
Who would like to feel the vibration?
Can you feel the balloon move?
Everyone, that's called a . . . vibration.

Let's look at these three pictures.
What do you see?

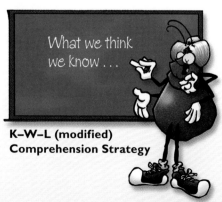

What we think we know . . .

K–W–L (modified)
Comprehension Strategy

69

Lap Book, Days 2 and 3

Getting to Know a Narrative Selection

Step 1. Turn to Lap Book 3, page 40, *Alice's Adventures in Wormland.*

Step 2. Read the Introduction. The Introduction helps students make connections with what they have learned.

Step 3. Read the story. Trace how the questions and comments direct attention to important story elements, knowledge, and vocabulary.

Step 4. At the conclusion, note how this narrative ends with a Story Summary. The retell is followed by a Pocket Chart sequencing activity. Then students make their own *Alice's Adventures in Wormland Retell Books,* so they can tell and retell the story about Alice and the little worm named Tierra.

The two new friends sat quietly sipping their tea and chatting.

Alice and Tierra had become . . . (friends).

After a bit, Alice said, "We learned in school that earthworms have no eyes."

Tierra said, "Wow! You are studying worms. I'm honored." Then Tierra tipped her yellow hat a bit, and Alice could see that Tierra had no eyes.

Everyone, did Tierra have eyes? (no)
Why not? (She is a worm.)

48

Lit Book Review

The Lit Book or Lap Book Review is always on Day 4. Although it is listed as "nonessential," the review is recommended. Young children love hearing the same story over and over. The process builds students' comfort with knowledge. Research findings support repeated reading of text with young children.

Teacher's Choice

This activity is specifically designed for you (or your students) to bring in another favorite book about a topic. See pages 100–101 for a list of suggested Read Alouds.

Enhance your read aloud experiences with one or more of the following preparations:

- Create ongoing lists of theme-related books.
- Create a center with theme-related books.
- Ask your librarian to create theme-related book tubs.
- Share literature lists with other teachers.
- Share lists with parents. Books make a wonderful gift.

Art Projects

The Art Projects in Units 1–8 and 10 are required because students use the projects in role-playing, as props during Read Alouds, or as decorations for the class apple tree. The remaining Art Projects are recommended but not required. These activities increase students' interest in a topic and build knowledge. Art Projects often require adult assistance. Have fun! Use your own topic-related Art Projects or those provided.

Art Project Chart • See what's included!

Unit 1	Unit 2	Unit 3	Unit 4
Apple Portrait Sing *At the Apple Tree* and add to the class apple tree.	**Binoculars** Use the binoculars when exploring your school.	**No Art Activity** Take a Listening Walk.	**Rhyming Flap Book**
Unit 5	**Unit 6**	**Unit 7**	**Unit 8**
Straw Hat Use as a prop with the Lap Book, Day 3 story.	**Stick Puppets** Use in interactive play with the Lap Book, Day 2 story.	**Spider** Sing *At the Apple Tree* and add to the class apple tree.	**Worm** Sing *At the Apple Tree* and add under the apple tree.
Unit 9	**Review (1–9)**	**Unit 10**	**Unit 11**
Zany Zoo Animal	**Play Dough Letters**	**Barnyard Animal Puppets** Use in interactive play with the Lap Book, Days 2 and 3 stories.	**Stand-Up Animal Friend**
Unit 12	**Unit 13**	**Unit 14**	**Unit 15**
Insect Sing *At the Apple Tree* and add around or under the class apple tree.	**Healthy Food Basket**	**Doctor's Bag**	**Safety Star**

Look ahead at the preparation notes in the front of each unit and in the left column of the teacher's guide in each unit. The notes suggest making a sample for students to see. Samples help students envision a finished product and inspire creativity. If you have helpers, create several samples, giving children the idea that each project will be special.

Unit 16	Unit 17	Unit 18	Short Vowel E
Swan Mask	Rhythm Shaker	Paper Doll	Play Dough Letters

Unit 19	Unit 20	Unit 21	Unit 22
Bee Assembly Sing *At the Apple Tree* and add around the class apple tree.	Flower Sing *At the Apple Tree* and add under the class apple tree.	Goose in the Grass	Seascape

Unit 23	Unit 24	Unit 25	Unit 26
Octopus Assembly	Classroom Quilt	Family Portrait	Apple Sing *At the Apple Tree* and add to the class apple tree.

Review (1–26)	Vowel Review		
Play Dough Letters	Summer Fun Games		

Songs

"Music makes a difference in people's lives.
It exalts the human spirit;
it enhances the quality of life."

(Housewright Symposium, 1999)

What's Included

Read Well K songs include jazzy alphabet songs, with their daily practice of letter names and sounds, and theme-based songs that build oral language patterns, rhyming skills, and vocabulary knowledge. Based on old favorite melodies—*Skip to My Lou, The Farmer in the Dell, Old Joe Clark, Baa Baa Black Sheep*—the theme-based songs will capture the fancy of your students while building content knowledge and interest in a topic.

Children will giggle as they wiggle through the *Wiggle Waggle Dance*—a song about bee communication. Following the flower unit, don't be surprised if you hear children singing about the life cycle of a plant, with *This Little Seed of Mine*.

As children learn about healthy food choices, they will sing "Don't want the jelly, jellybean junk food blues," the same lyrics sung by a blues-singing cat in the Lap Book story *The Jellybean Junk Food Blues*.

Jellybean Junk Food Blues
by Shelley V. Jones

Milk and fruit in the morning,
Veggie soup at noon,
Fish for my dinner,
And I'll grow real soon.
Don't want the jelly, jellybean junk food blues.
Don't want the jelly, jellybean junk food blues.

My dad likes bread.
My mom likes rice.
I think cereal
Would taste twice as nice!
Don't want the jelly, jellybean junk food blues.
Don't want the jelly, jellybean junk food blues.

Too much candy
Can be a big mistake,
'Cause your fingers get sticky
And your tummy aches.
Don't want the jelly, jellybean junk food blues.
Don't want the jelly, jellybean junk food blues.
Don't want the jelly, jellybean junk food blues.
Don't want the jelly, jellybean junk food blues.

REPETITION

Theme-related songs are repeated across the program with suggested extension activities to add creativity and variety. Review songs include those that build phonemic awareness and oral language. Watch for variations that encourage student creativity.

SKILLS

Rhythm, rhyme, and repetition: Throughout the program, *Read Well K* songs support instruction and provide repeated practice in oral language, phonemic awareness, phonics, vocabulary, comprehension, and fluency. The chart below reflects that support and repeated practice.

Component	RWK Songs	Unit																									
		1	2	3	4	5	6	7	8	9	10	11	12	13	14	15	16	17	18	19	20	21	22	23	24	25	26
Oral Language	Alphabet Songs	x	x	x	x	x	x	x	x	x	x	x	x	x	x	x	x	x	x	x	x	x	x	x	x		
	Thematic Songs	x	x	x			x																				
	Song Review			x	x			x	x				x							x	x						x
Phonemic Awareness	Alphabet Songs	x	x	x	x	x	x	x	x	x	x	x	x	x	x	x	x	x	x	x	x	x	x	x	x	x	x
	Thematic Songs			x	x			x	x	x	x	x															
	Song Review			x	x	x						x	x			x	x			x			x	x			
Letter Names	Alphabet Songs	x	x	x	x	x	x	x	x	x	x	x	x	x	x	x	x	x	x	x	x	x	x	x	x	x	x
	Thematic Songs																										x
	Song Review																										x
Phonics	Alphabet Songs	x	x	x	x	x	x	x	x	x	x	x	x	x	x	x	x	x	x	x	x	x	x	x	x	x	x
	Thematic Songs																										
	Song Review																										
Vocabulary	Alphabet Songs																										x
	Thematic Songs	x	x	x																	x	x	x	x			
	Song Review							x	x				x														
Comprehension	Alphabet Songs																										
	Thematic Songs	x	x	x			x	x	x	x	x	x		x		x	x	x	x	x	x	x	x	x	x		
	Song Review										x			x								x	x	x	x	x	x
Fluency	Alphabet Songs																										
	Thematic Songs		x	x																							
	Song Review			x	x			x						x						x			x				

ABC Scrapbook

Each unit includes making an ABC Scrapbook page. The activities are not required, but they combine to create a three-dimensional keepsake, complete with movable parts. If you do this year-long project, your students have a scrapbook they will treasure.

END-OF-YEAR CELEBRATION

Have students put their scrapbook pages in alphabetical order. Spiral bind the books to create a lasting memento of a joyful year.

Unit 1	Unit 2	Unit 3	Unit 4	Unit 5

Unit 6	Unit 7	Unit 8	Unit 9	Review (1–9)

Unit 10	Unit 11	Unit 12	Unit 13	Unit 14

Unit 15	Unit 16	Unit 17	Unit 18	Short Vowel E

Unit 19	Unit 20	Unit 21	Unit 22	Unit 23

Unit 24	Unit 25	Unit 26	Review (1–26)	Vowel Review

Journals

Journals can be a rich source of pride for young children. Every child can experience success. The recommended *Read Well K* journal topics review unit themes, encourage students to build memories, and revisit the background knowledge that was built in the previous units.

Journal Topics			
3	Cover	16	What Do You Want to Do When You Grow Up?
4	Special People	17	An Instrument for You
5	A Favorite Book	18	My Favorite Thing to Do
6	A Special Friend	E	My Favorite School Activity
7	Spiders	19	Bees
8	Worms	20	Flowers
9	A Favorite Place to Visit	21	My Favorite Nursery Rhyme
Rev	My Favorite Activity	22	Lobsters
10	Something I've Learned to Do	23	Octopuses
11	Animal Friends	24	A Special Relative
12	Things I Know About Insects	25	Family Celebrations
13	Favorite Healthy Foods	26	N/A
14	Good Friends Help Each Other	Rev	My Favorite Activity
15	People Who Can Help You	Rev	N/A

Children begin their journals by drawing theme-related pictures. If adult assistance is available, students also dictate a sentence or two about their drawings. Students with writing skills should be encouraged to label their drawings or to write sentences.

Journals, Best Guessing Spelling

Research Snapshot

" . . . phonemic awareness and spelling interact such that each enhances the other's development. Some ability to focus on a word's phonemic structure gets children started inventing spellings. Then, as they write, their skill at focusing on phonemes in words increases. In fact, Ehri and Wilce (1987) found that children's phonemic segmentation skills improved when they were taught to generate the phonetic spellings of words" (Griffith, 1991).

As your students' phonemic awareness and handwriting skills develop, *Read Well K* lessons encourage children to copy sentences and to compose their own sentences. As students' writing develops, you will demonstrate and guide students in Best Guess Spelling.

How to Teach Best Guess Spelling

Step 1. Have students help you segment a word into sounds.

Step 2. Write letters for the known sounds and a dash for unknown sounds.

Demonstrate writing each sound: My *fa-orit* ins-ct is a bee.

I want to write the word *favorite*. My *favorite* insect is a bee.
You can help me figure out the sounds.
Favorite is a big word, but we can figure it out.

What's the first sound in *favorite*? (/fff/)
Watch me write it.
What's the next sound in *faaavorite*? (/āāā/)
Watch me write it.

What's the next sound in *favvvorite*? (/vvv/)
I'm not sure how to write the sound /vvv/, so I'm going to write a little line called a dash.

The word is favorite. Now we have /fāv/.
What's the next sound in *favorite*? (/ōōō/)
Watch me write it.

What's the next sound in *favorite*? (/rrr/) Watch me write it.
Almost done! What's the next sound in *favorite*? (/ĭĭĭ/)
Watch me write it.

What's the last sound in *favorite*? (/t/)
Watch me write it.
My *favorite* insect is a bee. What big word did we spell? (favorite)
Wow! You just helped me write a big long word with Best Guess Spelling.
Here's how it's really spelled. We were very close.

Write "favorite" above the Best Guess Spelling.

favorite

fa-orit

Pocket Chart Activities

What's Included

Read Well K Pocket Chart activities are short but important lessons. They are used with:

- **Songs** (Days 1, 3, 4)
- **Pocket Chart Retells** (Day 3)
  The Day 3 Pocket Chart activities *prepare* students for the Day 3 Independent Work. The illustrations on the Pocket Chart Cards stir memories—helping students recall facts and retell the beginning, middle, and end of a Lap Book story before they begin the Bookmaking activity. One picture can bring a memory to life.

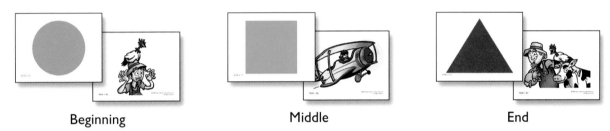

Beginning   Middle   End

- **Pocket Chart Sentence Scrambles** (Day 5)
  The Day 5 Pocket Chart Sentence Building activity prepares students for their sentence building Independent Work. By the end of the year, children will feel confident building sentences with a few sight words, pattern words, and picture words.

Skills Reviewed

Pocket Chart Cards

Component	RWK Pocket Chart Activities	1	2	3	4	5	6	7	8	9	10	11	12	13	14	15	16	17	18	19	20	21	22	23	24	25	26
Oral Language	Songs		x	x	x			x						x					x				x				
	Day 3																										
	Day 5							x	x		x		x		x		x		x		x						
Phonemic Awareness	Songs				x	x				x	x	x	x	x	x		x	x			x	x	x	x			
	Day 3																										
	Day 5				x		x																				
Vocabulary	Songs		x	x	x			x		x				x					x		x		x				
	Day 3												x														
	Day 5	x	x	x	x		x																				
Comprehension	Songs									x			x								x	x					
	Day 3				x		x	x	x	x	x	x	x	x	x	x	x	x	x	x	x	x	x	x		
	Day 5																										
Fluency	Day 5				x		x		x	x		x		x		x		x		x		x		x		x

79

Games

Have fun with the traditional games we've all played—*Duck, Duck, Goose*; *Simon Says*; rolling a ball; and tossing a bean bag—reformatted to provide more practice with letter names, sounds, rhyming words, and oral language patterns.

What's Included

- **At the Apple Tree**
  Review each other's names and practice an oral language pattern, as children sing and mount apples, spiders, bees, flowers, and letters on the class apple tree.

- **Ball Roll and Bean Bag**
  Roll a ball or toss a bean bag and practice introductions with "I'm [Mrs. B]." Use the same format later to identify rhyming words and beginning sounds.

- **Duck, Duck, Goose**
  Play variations of *Duck, Duck, Goose* with rhyming words in the game *Mouse, Mouse, House* and others.

- **Simon Says**
  This game provides practice with letters and sounds: Simon says, "Touch the word that begins with /mmm/." Game Boards are provided in the appendix.

Skills Reviewed

Games

Component	Unit																													
	1	2	3	4	5	6	7	8	9	R	10	11	12	13	14	15	16	17	18	E	19	20	21	22	23	24	25	26	R	R
Oral Language	x	x	x				x	x					x								x	x						x		
Phonemic Awareness				x	x	x			x	x	x	x	x	x	x	x	x	x	x					x	x	x	x		x	
Letter Names									x	x										x									x	x
Phonics									x	x										x									x	x

Stretch and Shrink

Stretch and Shrink is an oral exercise, occurring in the first six Whole Class units. This *Read Well* phonemic awareness activity primes students for sounding out words. In the *Name Game*, you stretch out a student's name, then the class shrinks the name.

What's Included

Unit	Stretch and Shrink Game	Word(s) for Stretch and Shrink
1	Name Game	Student names [/Ăăănnn/, Ann]
2	Name Game: How Are You? I'm Fine	Student names; /IIImmm/, I'm
3	What Do You See/Hear?	/III/, I
4	What Are You Doing?	/IIImmm/, I'm
5	How Are You?	/IIImmm/, I'm
6	Will You Be My Friend?, Will You Eat With Me?	/III/, I; /mmmēēē/, me

Getting to Know Stretch and Shrink

Step 1. Skim the directions for the Unit 3, Day 1 Stretch and Shrink.

Step 2. Read the text below. The boxed notes highlight the explicit instruction steps.

DEMONSTRATE when students are first learning the task. Show students how to stretch out the word smoothly.

GUIDE students with your voice. Have students stretch out the word with you.

Then have students shrink up the word with you.

PROVIDE INDEPENDENT PRACTICE by having students shrink the word without your voice.

❶ Show and explain Stretch and Shrink with "I."

Today, we're going to play another Stretch and Shrink game with the word *I*.

I'll call on someone and ask "What do you see?"

[Lisa], what do you see?   (a [chair])

Good. Say "I see a [chair]."   (I see a [chair].)

Demonstrate stretching "I."

Listen to me stretch out *I*.

Start with your hands together, then move them apart.   /III/

Everyone, use the hand motions and stretch out *I* with me.   /III/

Now let's shrink it up.

Move your hands back together as you and the students shrink "I."   I

❷ Play the game, asking several students "What do you see?"

• Use the Stretch and Shrink hand motions throughout.

[Natasha], what do you see?   (I see [a clock].)

That's great. [Natasha] used the word *I*.

• Before each repetition, demonstrate the smooth slow stretching of the word "I."

Listen while I stretch out *I*.

Move your hands apart while stretching "I" with your voice.   /III/

Everyone, use the hand motions and stretch out *I* with me.   /III/

Now *you* shrink it up.

Move your hands back together as students shrink "I."   (I)

81

Stretch and Shrink (continued)

Step 3. Practice Stretch and Shrink with a colleague, using the examples below. The examples use the same coding of quick and continuous sounds you will find in your teacher's guides. Continuous sounds are listed with repeating letters (/mmm/), indicating that you sustain the sounds for about two seconds. Quick sounds are listed once (/d/), indicating that you merge the quick sounds with the next sound.

STRETCH AND SHRINK PRACTICE WORDS

I–III–I

One continuous breath

I'm—IIImmm—I'm

Say   Stretch   Shrink

me—mmmeee—me

WORKING TOWARD MASTERY

Play phonemic awareness games with Stretch and Shrink.

Catch Me If You Can

To play this game, purposely make the same error stretching out a word and ask students to catch you if they can. Say something like:

I'm going to play another Stretch and Shrink game—*Catch Me If You Can*.
Thumbs up if I stretch out smoothly.
Thumbs down if you catch me stopping between sounds.
Listen. /mmmăăă/•/nnn/

[Malika], why did you put your thumbs down? What did I do?
(You stopped.)
That's right. I stopped after /mmmăăă/. It should be /mmmăăănnn/.

Everyone, stretch out *man* with me. /mmmăăănnn/
Shrink it up. (man)

Big Stretches

Using a stopwatch, have a contest to see how long students can stretch a word. Periodically, provide individual coaching for children with difficulties.

Smooth and Bumpy Blending

In Smooth and Bumpy Blending, children learn the difference between blending sounds smoothly and blending sounds while stopping or pausing between each letter/sound association.

Smooth Blending: /mmmēēē/–me

Bumpy Blending: /mmm/•/ēēē/–me

Smooth Blending paves the way to early and easy success in sounding out words.

SMOOTH AND BUMPY BLENDING CONCEPTS

In *Read Well K* Smooth and Bumpy Blending, students are introduced to little Hector Ant. Hector goes bump, bump, bump when he drives his truck with a flat tire, but he sails smoothly along when he rides in his glider. Using this concept, students practice Smooth and Bumpy Blending by bumping along with Hector in his truck or gliding along with Hector in his glider. Students begin with one-sound blending, then graduate to two- and three-sound blending.

Read Well Smooth and Bumpy Blending follows the three important steps in explicit instruction. See if you can fill in the blank.

a. Demonstrate

b. Guide practice

c. _____

SCRIPTS MODEL SCAFFOLDING

Though you will not read the script during instruction, scripts are scaffolded to model how to gradually fade demonstrations and guided practice across lessons. You will teach diagnostically, gradually dropping your demonstration and guidance as students are able to blend more and more independently. In the scripts, demonstration is dropped after the first two lessons. Guided practice is dropped after four lessons, and all subsequent lessons begin with group and individual practice, without your voice.

Special note: It is important to move back to demonstration and guided practice whenever children need assistance.

Answer Key: c. Provide group and individual turns, without your voice

Smooth and Bumpy Blending (*continued*)

Getting to Know Smooth Blending With a Beginning Quick Sound

Step 1. Read the script below for the Unit 11, Day 4 Smooth and Bumpy Blending activity. Pay special attention to the boxed note in the left column. After reading the note, you should be able to explain why you skip the <u>d</u> and loop directly to the <u>a</u> in "dad."

Step 2. Locate Blending Card 18. Practice teaching how to blend with /d/.

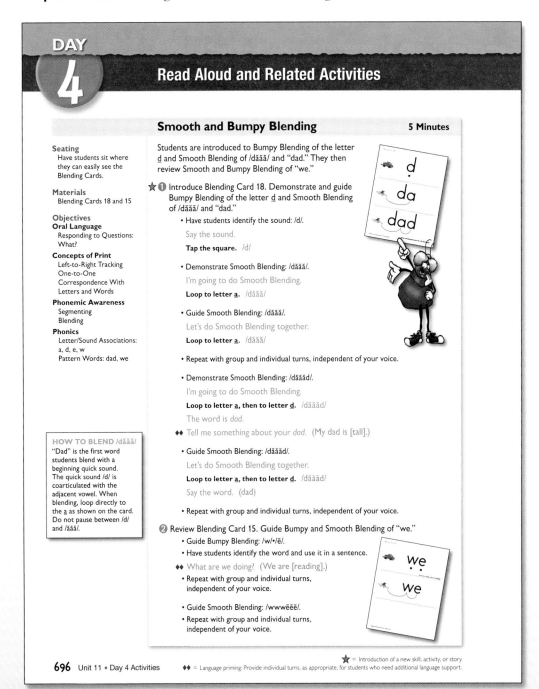

DAY 4

Read Aloud and Related Activities

Smooth and Bumpy Blending   5 Minutes

Seating
Have students sit where they can easily see the Blending Cards.

Materials
Blending Cards 18 and 15

Objectives
Oral Language
Responding to Questions: What?
Concepts of Print
Left-to-Right Tracking
One-to-One Correspondence With Letters and Words
Phonemic Awareness
Segmenting
Blending
Phonics
Letter/Sound Associations: a, d, e, w
Pattern Words: dad, we

Students are introduced to Bumpy Blending of the letter d and Smooth Blending of /dăăă/ and "dad." They then review Smooth and Bumpy Blending of "we."

⭐ ❶ Introduce Blending Card 18. Demonstrate and guide Bumpy Blending of the letter <u>d</u> and Smooth Blending of /dăăă/ and "dad."
 • Have students identify the sound: /d/.
   Say the sound.
   Tap the square. /d/

 • Demonstrate Smooth Blending: /dăăă/.
   I'm going to do Smooth Blending.
   Loop to letter a. /dăăă/

 • Guide Smooth Blending: /dăăă/.
   Let's do Smooth Blending together.
   Loop to letter a. /dăăă/

 • Repeat with group and individual turns, independent of your voice.

 • Demonstrate Smooth Blending: /dăăăd/.
   I'm going to do Smooth Blending.
   Loop to letter a, then to letter d. /dăăăd/
   The word is *dad*.
◆◆ Tell me something about your *dad*. (My dad is [tall].)

 • Guide Smooth Blending: /dăăăd/.
   Let's do Smooth Blending together.
   Loop to letter a, then to letter d. /dăăăd/
   Say the word. (dad)

 • Repeat with group and individual turns, independent of your voice.

❷ Review Blending Card 15. Guide Bumpy and Smooth Blending of "we."
 • Guide Bumpy Blending: /w/•/ē/.
 • Have students identify the word and use it in a sentence.
◆◆ What are *we* doing? (We are [reading].)
 • Repeat with group and individual turns, independent of your voice.

 • Guide Smooth Blending: /wwwēēē/.
 • Repeat with group and individual turns, independent of your voice.

> **HOW TO BLEND** /dăăă/
> "Dad" is the first word students blend with a beginning quick sound. The quick sound /d/ is coarticulated with the adjacent vowel. When blending, loop directly to the <u>a</u> as shown on the card. Do not pause between /d/ and /ăăă/.

⭐ = Introduction of a new skill, activity, or story
◆◆ = Language priming: Provide individual turns, as appropriate, for students who need additional language support.

White Board • Dictate, Copy, and Draw

Read Well K White Board activities provide another tool for working on fine motor skills, drawing, and handwriting. Children gently and systematically learn how to listen for sounds, count sounds, and write the letters that the sounds represent. With these skills, your students will approach writing tasks with ease and enjoyment. Be sure to do each lesson consecutively.

MAKING WHITE BOARDS

Children can use paper rather than white boards for these activities; however, young children love the novelty of the white boards. You may wish to have your PTA donate shower board and markers. Home supply stores carry the inexpensive white shower board and will often cut the board into appropriate student lap sizes. The edges of the boards can be sanded by parent volunteers or older students. Socks make great washable erasers.

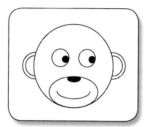

MANAGEMENT

The biggest challenge in using white boards is managing the materials. Here are a few tips:

- Schedule White Board activities so that the boards can be carefully laid out in advance.

- The first White Board activity occurs at Unit 2 on Day 5. Important procedures are included for teaching students how to manage the white boards and markers.

- Teach students a routine for picking up the white boards, markers, and erasers. As you pick up the boards, student helpers can follow with a tub for the markers and another for the erasers. While materials are being picked up, keep everyone engaged by singing a counting song.

> **COUNTING SONG**
>
> One little, two little, three little white boards,
>
> Four little, five little, six little white boards,
>
> Seven little, eight little, nine little white boards,
>
> Ten little white boards all picked up.
>
> Eleven little, twelve little, thirteen little white boards . . .

DICTATION

Read Well K includes four basic types of dictation: sound, pattern word, Tricky Word, and sentence.

White Board • Dictate, Copy, and Draw (continued)

Getting to Know Sound Dictation

Step 1. Skim the directions for the Unit 3, Day 2 White Board activity.

Step 2. Follow the bulleted items to identify the basic steps in the process. See if you can fill in the answers below:

a. Students identify the _____ at the beginning of a word.

b. You _____ writing the letter/sound association.

c. Students identify the sound at the beginning of the word again.

d. You dictate the sound, and students _____ the sound.

e. Provide additional _____.

DAY 2 — Read Aloud and Related Activities

White Board (continued)

★❸ Have students identify and write the new sound:

/ăăă/ at the beginning of **a**nt with small letter <u>a</u>
/ăăă/ at the beginning of **A**pple with capital letter <u>A</u>

White Board (continued)

★❸ Have students identify and write the new sound:

/ăăă/ at the beginning of **a**nt with small letter <u>a</u>
/ăăă/ at the beginning of **A**pple with capital letter <u>A</u>

You're going to learn how to do something very grown-up.
You are going to learn how to spell.

- Have students identify the sound they hear at the beginning of the word.
  What sound do you hear at the beginning of *a*nt? (/ăăă/)

- Demonstrate writing the letter for the sound.
  Watch me write /ăăă/ with a small letter <u>a</u>.

- Have students identify the sound they hear at the beginning of the word again.
  What sound do you hear at the beginning of *a*nt? (/ăăă/)

- Dictate the sound and have students write the letter for the sound.
  Write /ăăă/ with the small letter <u>a</u>.

- Repeat with /ăăă/ at the beginning of "Apple."
- Provide additional practice with each letter, as appropriate.

❹ Have students draw circles and make happy faces on their white boards to celebrate their ability to spell /ăăă/ at the beginning of "ant" and "Apple."

❺ Have students erase their white boards. Then encourage students to write or draw something of their choice.

PUTTING AWAY MATERIALS

While materials are being picked up, have the class sing a counting song or practice counting.

COUNTING SONG

One little, two little, three little white boards,

Four little, five little, six little white boards,

Seven little, eight little, nine little white boards,

Ten little white boards all picked up.

Eleven little, twelve little, thirteen white boards . . .

Answer Key: a. sound, b. demonstrate, d. copy, e. practice

Getting to Know Pattern Word Dictation

Step 1. Skim the directions for the Unit 7, Day 5 White Board activity.

Step 2. Follow the bulleted items to identify the basic steps in the process. See if you can fill in the answers.

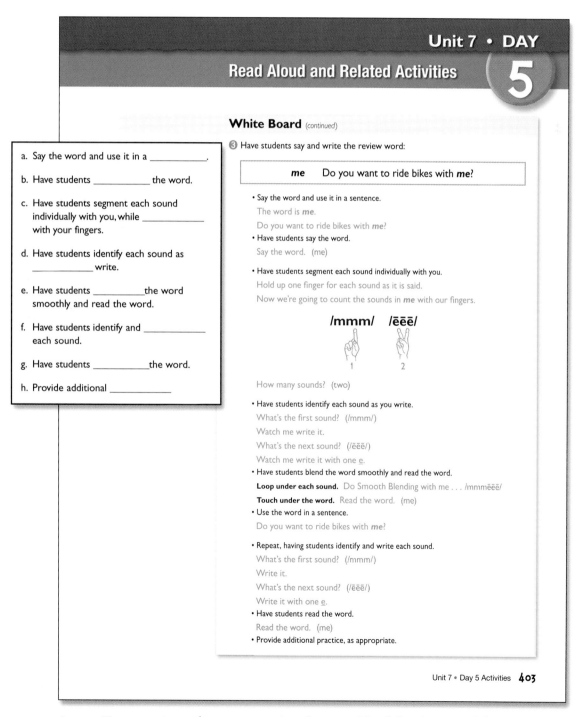

Unit 7 • DAY

5

Read Aloud and Related Activities

White Board (continued)

❸ Have students say and write the review word:

> **me**   Do you want to ride bikes with **me**?

• Say the word and use it in a sentence.
  The word is **me**.
  Do you want to ride bikes with **me**?
• Have students say the word.
  Say the word. (me)
• Have students segment each sound individually with you.
  Hold up one finger for each sound as it is said.
  Now we're going to count the sounds in **me** with our fingers.

/mmm/   /ēēē/

  1   2

  How many sounds? (two)

• Have students identify each sound as you write.
  What's the first sound? (/mmm/)
  Watch me write it.
  What's the next sound? (/ēēē/)
  Watch me write it with one e.
• Have students blend the word smoothly and read the word.
  Loop under each sound. Do Smooth Blending with me . . . /mmmēēē/
  Touch under the word. Read the word. (me)
• Use the word in a sentence.
  Do you want to ride bikes with **me**?

• Repeat, having students identify and write each sound.
  What's the first sound? (/mmm/)
  Write it.
  What's the next sound? (/ēēē/)
  Write it with one e.
• Have students read the word.
  Read the word. (me)
• Provide additional practice, as appropriate.

Unit 7 • Day 5 Activities **403**

Boxed note (left):

a. Say the word and use it in a _____.

b. Have students _____ the word.

c. Have students segment each sound individually with you, while _____ with your fingers.

d. Have students identify each sound as _____ write.

e. Have students _____the word smoothly and read the word.

f. Have students identify and _____ each sound.

g. Have students _____the word.

h. Provide additional _____

Answer Key: a. sentence, b. say, c. counting, d. you, e. blend, f. write, g. read, h. practice

87

White Board • Dictate, Copy, and Draw (*continued*)

Getting to Know Tricky Word and Sentence Dictation

SPELLING BY LETTERS

Tricky Words are irregular words—those that have one or more letters that do not represent the most common letter/sound associations. *Read Well K* dictation includes the following irregular words: is (Unit 14), the (Unit 17), a (Unit 19), was (Unit 22), have (Unit 24).

In *Read Well*, Tricky Word introductions have been tailored to match the skills children have learned and to reflect the degree to which the word includes regular letter/sound associations. Preview each script before teaching.

SENTENCE DICTATION

Read Well K begins sentence dictation in Unit 9. Students write a short sentence using the pattern words and Tricky Words they have practiced. The steps in sentence dictation follow the steps in pattern word dictation. The following script provides an outline for sentence dictation. Try filling in the script that is missing with your own words.

1. **Say the sentence.** You're going to write the sentence "See Sam."

2. **Have students say the sentence.** _____

3. **Segment the sounds in the first word with students.**

   We're going to count the sounds in the first word, see, with our fingers.
   /sss/•/ēēē/
   How many sounds? (two)

4. **Write the first word, having students identify each sound as you write.**

   What's the first sound in *see*?
   Watch me write it with a capital <u>S</u>.
   _____ ?

   Watch me write it with two small letter <u>e</u>'s.

5. **Have students blend the word and read it.**

   _____ .

   _____ .

6. **Dictate the word, having students identify each sound as they write.**

   What's the first sound? Write it with a _____ .
   _____ ? Write it with _____ .

7. **Repeat steps 3–6 for each word in the sentence.**

8. **Have students read the sentence and put a period at the end.**

   _____ .

   _____ .

How to Use Independent Work

Read Well K Independent Work meets multiple goals and objectives, the first of which is to provide children with worthwhile work that they can manage on their own. See page 48 for information about how to use the first few weeks of school to teach your children this important skill. In addition, Read Well K Independent Work provides:

- An important review of phonological skills, phonics, and comprehension
- A daily Family Connection to encourage parents to talk with their children about what they have learned

Skills Reviewed

Independent Work

Component	Letter Trace	Letter Book	Bookmaking	Sorting, Sentence Writing	Sentence Scrambles, Jigsaw Puzzles, Little Books
Phonemic Awareness		x	x	x	x
Letter Names	x	x		x	
Handwriting	x	x		x	
Comprehension			x	x	

What's Included

Day 1 • Letter Trace

Students trace letters, color pictures, and find letters, thus providing another opportunity to practice the newest letter/sound association and to review previously introduced letters. With Letter Trace, children discuss the letter they are studying and name review letters.

> **SAMPLE FAMILY CONNECTION, LETTER TRACE**
>
> Instructions for family members: Ask your child to tell you about this page. "What letter are you studying?" (<u>h</u>) • "What in the picture begins with <u>h</u>?" (house and horses) • "What letters are at the bottom of the page?" (<u>e</u>, <u>a</u>, <u>e</u>)

Day 2 • Letter Book

Students trace letters, practice sound discrimination, color pictures, read sentences, and discuss their books with family members.

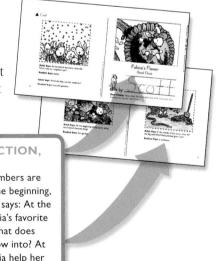

Day 3 • Bookmaking

Students make class books, rhyming books, retell books, fact books, and books about family and friends. A special script to prompt retells is included—perfect for conversations with family members.

> **SAMPLE FAMILY CONNECTION, RETELL BOOK**
>
> Discussion questions for family members are provided under pictures showing the beginning, middle, and end of the story. Adult says: At the beginning of the story, what is Felicia's favorite thing? In the middle of the story, what does the big seed that Felicia planted grow into? At the end of the story, what did Felicia help her neighbors to have?

How to Use Independent Work

Day 4 • Sorting or Sentence Writing

Students sort pictures into categories (/mmm/ things, not /mmm/ things). In later units, they trace and/or complete phrases and sentences to make a small book.

Day 5 • Sentence Scramble, Jigsaw Puzzle, or Little Book

Students cut out, color, and glue together Jigsaw Puzzles or Sentence Scrambles. In other units, they assemble Little Books. Children practice rhyming, beginning sounds, onsets and rimes, and sentence fluency.

> **SAMPLE FAMILY CONNECTION**
> Point to the words and have your child read each sentence with you. Next, have your child point to the words and read the sentence. Congratulate your child on his or her ability to read the sentence.

How to Use Homework

RWK provides many options for inviting parents to participate in this exciting year. In addition to making family connections with discussions about completed Independent Work, Whole Class includes one Homework page per unit. (See Whole Class Activities, Homework blackline masters.) Each Whole Class Homework activity is a letter/sound page that can be done independently or with family members.

For each unit, students draw or cut out pictures and write or cut out words that begin with the unit's newly introduced letter.

ESTABLISH HOME SHARING ROUTINES

- Select a regular day of the week when *RWK* Whole Class Homework is sent home with students. Homework can be sent home at the beginning, middle, or end of a unit.
- Provide a homework folder for each student to carry to and from home.

WORK WITH FAMILY MEMBERS

- Explain the homework routine during conferences and in a beginning-of-the-year letter.
- Encourage parents to assist their children, as needed.
- Ask parents to watch for the Whole Class Homework on a specific day.
- Suggest that completed homework be placed where it won't be forgotten—e.g., in the child's backpack, next to the door, etc.

CELEBRATE HOMEWORK COMPLETION

- Greet children at the door. Personally collect homework and congratulate each child. A *quick* compliment goes a long way in encouraging children to do their personal best.
- Optional: Make a class book of the completed Whole Class Homework for each unit—e.g., *The Letter A Book*. Add to a class library. Have each child take a book home at the end of the year.
- Provide a time early in the day for children to complete work. Circumstances can make it difficult for students to complete their homework.
- If there is a pattern of incomplete work, have the child work with a parent helper or an instructional assistant before going home. Have the child take the assignment home, whether it's all or partially done. This allows the child to practice getting work home and back and provides an opportunity to build good habits through success.

How to Use Language Priming

Students with delayed language skills and/or students who are learning English need individual opportunities to practice speaking. Additional language support can be provided during every *Read Well K* activity. Watch the Oral Language Objectives in the teacher's guides for question/response patterns and see the examples marked with diamonds (◆◆) in most activities. As children recognize language patterns, they will more willingly participate in conversation. The goal is for students to use English spontaneously.

Teach instructional assistants, parent volunteers, and older students to use the programmed language patterns from the teacher's guides. Examples are shown in the chart below. (See page 94 for a sample teaching script.)

Oral Language

Activity	Language Priming Examples
Alphabet Routines (Days 1–5) Review what is on the unit and previous unit posters.	What do you see on the poster? (dogs) Where are the dogs? (on a doghouse)
Daily Story Reading (Days 1–5) Review the (Lit Book or Lap Book) story and ask comprehension questions.	Who is the story about? (Sam) What are some things we know about Sam? (He has red hair, freckles, no front teeth, and a great big smile. He is short.)
Art Project (Day 1) Practice identifying the Art Project.	What is this? (a spider) Yes, this is a . . . (spider). Say the whole sentence. (This is a spider.)
Pocket Chart Cards With Songs (Days 1, 3, 4) Practice identifying the Pocket Chart Cards.	What is this? or What do you see? (a cow) Yes, a red cow. What do you see? (a blue horse . . .)
Journals (Day 3) Talk with the student about his or her picture. Have the student dictate a sentence about his or her picture.	Tell me about your picture. What is this? or Who is this? (That's me and that's my friend.) What are you doing? (helping each other) What are you helping each other do? (pick up toys)

(continued)

How to Use Language Priming (*continued*)

Oral Language (*continued*)

Activity	Language Priming Examples
Letter Book (Day 2) Practice identifying pictures, sounds, picture words, and words.	What letter are we studying? (s) What sound does it make? (/sss/) What is this? (a sun) I hear /sss/ at the beginning of ssssun. What sound do you hear at the beginning of sssun? (/sss/) What is this? (a snake)
Pocket Chart Cards/Bookmaking (Day 3) Talk with the student about the Pocket Chart Cards or his or her book.	Who is the story about? or Who is this? (Old MacDonald) At the beginning of the story, what was Old MacDonald's problem? (There was too much noise.) In the middle of the story, Old MacDonald went in search of peace and . . . (quiet). At the end of the story, what did Old MacDonald miss? (his home and the noise)
Jigsaw Puzzle (Day 5) Practice identifying pictures, sounds, picture words, and words.	Tell me the first sound. (/sss/) Tell me the next sound. (/ēēē/) Do Smooth Blending. (/sssēēē/) Read the word. (see) Look at the picture word. What is the picture word? ({see}) It's a match!
Pocket Chart Cards/Sentence Scrambles/Little Books (Day 5) Practice identifying pictures, picture words, and words. Practice reading sentences.	What is this? (a bike) Yes, let's read the sentence together. {See} the {bike}. Now you read the sentence. ({See} the {bike}.)

Adult Helpers or Older Students

Take advantage of adult helpers and older students who are available to help in your classroom. With a minimum of instruction, they can help your children build language. For example, using review ABC Poem Posters, you could say something like:

I'd like you to talk with students about their ABC Poem Posters.

For each poster, please ask them "What do you see on the poster?"

They should reply "[dogs]."

Then ask them "Where are the [dogs]?"

They should reply "[on a doghouse]." Using the phrase is important.

Help anyone who has difficulty with the answers.

Say "Oh, the [dogs are . . . on a doghouse]. Where are they?"

They should reply "[on a doghouse]."

Say "That's right! They are [on a doghouse]."

Appendix

In this section:

Setting Up and Organizing Materials

Whole Class Set-Up

Locate the following materials to set up your classroom. Materials that need to be easily visible to all students are marked with an asterisk.

Read Well K Materials	Set-Up
☐ *ABC Wall Cards	Mount the cards with only the letters showing. Place cards low enough so the children can see the illustrations when the cards are turned over.
☐ *ABC Poem Posters	Mount the poster for the unit on a bulletin board. Keep review posters close by.
☐ *Whole Class Blending Cards (vertical orientation)	Decide where you will keep the cards—on a bulletin board, in a basket or box, etc.
☐ Pocket Chart Cards	Place in a box or basket.

School Materials	Set-Up
☐ CD Player	
☐ *Pocket Chart	
☐ Apple Tree Bulletin Board	See page 99.
☐ White/Chalk Boards, Markers, Erasers	If you don't have small white/chalk boards, see page 85 for how to make white boards. Socks can be used for erasers. (Paper can also be used.)

Note: Ask staff members to save toilet-paper tubes. You will need two tubes per student for the Unit 2 Art Project Binoculars. Don't miss this terrific beginning-of-the-year activity!

Getting Reading

Be prepared. It will ease your mind and provide you with a relaxing year. The following suggestions may help you organize.

Read Well K Materials	Preparation/Organization
☐ Placement Inventory (blackline masters in the *Assessment Manual*)	Set up a Placement Notebook for each person assisting with the Placement Inventory. Include copies of the Placement Inventory (*Assessment Manual* pages 29–37) and Student Placement Record Parts 1 and 2.
☐ Lit Books	Place Lit Books in the hanging files by unit. See pages 100 and 101.
☐ Independent Work (blackline masters or *My Activity Books*) The most important activities are: Day 1, Letter Trace; Day 3, Bookmaking; and Day 5, Jigsaw Puzzles, Sentence Scrambles, and Little Books.	Blackline Master Option: • Set up five files for each unit (Independent Work: Days 1, 2, 3, 4, 5). • Send BLMs to be copied. File when returned. See preparation instructions in the BLM packages. *Note:* The Letter Book BLMs are double-sided for Units 1–25. Unit 26 requires three single-sided copies for children to cut and collate into a small ABC Book.

Read Well K Materials	Preparation/Organization
❑ Art Projects	• Determine which projects you will do. Units 1–8 and Unit 10 are required. (See pages 72 and 73 for a full visual display.) • Make a file folder for each Art Project by unit. • Send the Art Project BLMs to be copied. File when returned. • See page 98 for materials you may wish to gather in advance.
❑ ABC Scrapbook	• Determine whether you will do the *RWK* ABC Scrapbook. (See page 76.) • Set up a file folder for each unit. • Send the ABC Scrapbook BLMs to be copied. File when returned. • Determine how you will store the finished pages—in notebooks for reuse in subsequent years, in file folders for each child, etc. • Determine whether and how you will bind the books at the end of the year. • See the next page for a list of special materials you may wish to gather in advance.
❑ Whole Class Homework (blackline masters)	• Determine whether you will do the *RWK* Whole Class Homework. (See page 92.) • Set up a Homework file folder for each unit. • Send the Homework BLMs to be copied. File when returned.
❑ Journal Activities (blackline masters)	• Determine whether you will do the Journals. (See page 77.) • Make your own journals or use the BLMs provided in the appendix of this manual. • Send for printing: One Journal cover per student, 20 copies per student of page 115 (plain) *or* 116 (slanted) for the first 18 units and two review units, and nine double-sided copies of pages 117 and 118 per student for Units 19 through Review (1–26). (If your students enter kindergarten with fairly advanced skills, you may wish to use the double-sided pages before Unit 19.)
❑ Simon Says (blackline masters)	• Make a file folder for each game by unit (Units 9, 14, and 17, Short Vowel E and Review, Review 1–26). • Send Game Board BLMs to be copied. (See pages 110–113 for BLMs.) Laminate, file, and use the games across several years.
❑ Work Samples	• Make samples of Independent Work, Homework, Art Projects, and ABC Scrapbook Art. *You may wish to schedule a parent work party for these. (See page 98.)* • Keep samples in files.
❑ Lit Books	Begin copying questions and comments for the Lit Books into the books. Hand copy the questions from the lessons onto sticky notes.

School Materials	Preparation/Organization
❑ Hanging File Folders	Set up 30 hanging folders—a folder for each numbered unit 1–26, plus Review (1–9), Short Vowel E and Review (1–26), Review (1–26), and Vowel Review (1–26).

Art Materials Needed

Unit	Art Project	ABC Scrapbook Art
2	toilet-paper tubes (2 per student)	colored tissue paper
3		red paper
4		craft sticks (one per student) and colored paper
5	Optional: raffia	
6	craft sticks (3 per student)	colored paper or feathers (2 or 3 per student)
7		glitter, yarn or string, tape
8		yarn
9	colored paper, Optional: feathers, plastic eyes, buttons	felt or yarn
Rev	play dough: flour, salt, cooking oil, water, food coloring	Optional: glitter
10	craft sticks	
11	Optional: paper scraps	
12	colored paper (11x17)	
13	construction paper (one piece per student)	
14	yarn (one 24-inch length of yarn per student)	yarn, tissue paper
15	yarn (one 36-inch length of yarn per student), hole punch	glitter
16	craft sticks (one per student) Optional: crepe paper	colored paper, Optional: paper clips, buttons, beads, washers, plastic pieces
17	paper strips or crepe paper strips, dry beans (10 per student), Optional: paper plates (one per student)	
18		paper bags
E	play dough: flour, salt, cooking oil, water, food coloring	Optional: glitter
19	Optional: black and yellow felt, pipe cleaners	
20	yarn	paper baking cups
21	craft sticks, cups, soil, grass seed	brown paper, green paper
22	blue watercolors, paint brushes, cups for water	
23		paper-punch holes, Optional: hole reinforcements
24	yarn	cloth quilt squares
25		coffee filters, water colors, or felt-tip markers
26	yarn	
Rev	play dough: flour, salt, cooking oil, water, food coloring	
Vowel Rev	Optional: sealable plastic sandwich bags or envelopes labeled with students' names (one per student)	Optional: glitter

Optional: Parent Work Party, Before School Starts

Parents of kindergarten children often enjoy contributing to their children's program and becoming acquainted with you and your classroom. Here's a few ways to get them involved:

- Schedule a parent work party before school starts to set up projects and make samples of Independent Work, Scrapbook Art, Art Projects, and Homework.
- Send completed Independent Work home on a nightly basis. Ask parents to follow the "Dear Family" directions and adult prompts on the retell projects (Day 3 Independent Work).

Whole Class Apple Tree

The class apple tree is a spin-off from the coconut tree in *Chicka Chicka Boom Boom*. The tree is the center of activities throughout the year. Make a big bulletin board apple tree with removable leaves. Use materials of your choice.

Across the Year With the Apple Tree	
UNIT 1 • Day 1 Song	Children decorate the apple tree with the alphabet while singing the get-acquainted song *At the Apple Tree.*
UNIT 1 • Day 1 Art Project **UNIT 1 • Day 2** Song	Children draw their portraits in an apple. Children decorate the class apple tree with their apple portraits while singing, "[Trina] is at the apple tree, [Trina] is at the apple tree . . ."
Creative Extension	Use the binoculars from the Unit 2 Art Project. Ask children "Who do you see?"
UNIT 7 • Day 1 Art Project **UNIT 7 • Day 2** Song	Children make Art Project spiders. Children sing *At the Apple Tree* while hanging spiders on the tree.
UNIT 8 • Day 1 Art Project **UNIT 8 • Day 2** Song	Children make Art Project worms. Children sing *At the Apple Tree* while placing their worms underground, below the tree.
Autumn Extension	Have children sing the get-acquainted song *At the Apple Tree* while placing pumpkins under the tree.
Autumn Extension	Remove the leaves from the apple tree as you discuss the changing weather and seasons. (You may wish to save the leaves for the spring.)
Winter Extension	Have children make snowflakes and hang them from the tree limbs. Discuss the winter season. Make connections with your own climate. Explain that apple trees grow where it snows in the winter.
Winter/Spring Extension	Make a beehive and place it in the tree. If it's still winter, explain that the bees are dormant.
UNIT 19 • Day 1 Art Project **UNIT 19 • Day 2** Song	Students make Art Project bees. Children sing *At the Apple Tree* while placing bees in and around the tree (or hive).
Early Spring Extension	Add leaves, then blossoms. Explain that the blossoms will become apples.
UNIT 20 • Day 1 Art Project **UNIT 20 • Day 2** Song	Children mount their Art Project flowers under the tree, creating a colorful bed of flowers growing in the soil cultivated by the worms.
UNIT 26 • Day 3	To parallel the Lap Book story, children get to be detectives in the *Case of the Missing X.* Place a clue in the apple tree.
UNIT 26 • Day 1 Art Project and Song	Remove the blossoms and hang children's three-dimensional apple art in the apple tree. Sing *At the Apple Tree.*

Lit Books

Titles in red are included in the *Read Well K* Children's Literature Set. All other titles are suggested read alouds.

Unit	Title	Author	Genre
1	Chicka Chicka Boom Boom	Bill Martin, Jr. and John Archambault	Fiction • Rhyming Narrative
	Miss Bindergarten Gets Ready for Kindergarten	Joseph Slate	Fiction • Narrative
	The Berenstain Bears Go to School	Stan and Jan Berenstain	Fiction • Narrative
	A My Name Is . . .	Alice Lyne	Alphabet Book
	Kipper's A to Z	Mick Inkpen	Alphabet Book
2	Brown Bear, Brown Bear, What Do You See?	Bill Martin, Jr.	Fiction • Repetitive Narrative
	I Went Walking	Sue Williams	Fiction • Narrative
	I Took a Walk	Henry Cole	Fiction • Narrative
3	The Listening Walk	Paul Showers	Fiction • Narrative
	Polar Bear, Polar Bear, What Do You Hear?	Bill Martin, Jr.	Fiction • Repetitive Narrative
	The Ear Book	Al Perkins	Fiction • Narrative
4	Green Eggs and Ham	Dr. Seuss	Fiction • Rhyming Narrative
	One Fish, Two Fish, Red Fish, Blue Fish	Dr. Seuss	Fiction • Rhyming Narrative
5	Caps For Sale	Esphyr Slobodkina	Fiction • Narrative
	Five Little Monkeys Jumping on the Bed	Eileen Christelow	Fiction • Repetitive Rhyme
6	Friends	Helme Heine	Fiction • Narrative
	Pumpkin Soup	Helen Cooper	Fiction • Narrative
7	The Very Busy Spider	Eric Carle	Fiction • Narrative
	The Itsy Bitsy Spider	Iza Trapani	Fiction • Rhyming Narrative
8	Wonderful Worms	Linda Glaser	Nonfiction • Expository
	The Early Bird	Richard Scarry	Fiction • Narrative
9	The Baby Beebee Bird	Diane Redfield Massie	Fiction • Narrative
	If Anything Ever Goes Wrong at the Zoo	Mary Jean Hendrick	Fiction • Narrative
10	The Cow That Went OINK	Bernard Most	Fiction • Narrative
	Cock-A-Doodle-Moo!	Bernand Most	Fiction • Narrative
11	The Adventures of Taxi Dog	Debra and Sal Barracca	Fiction • Narrative
	The Great Gracie Chase: Stop That Dog!	Cynthia Rylant	Fiction • Narrative
12	Two Bad Ants	Chris Van Allsburg	Fiction • Narrative
	The Very Quiet Cricket	Eric Carle	Fiction • Narrative
13	The Berenstain Bears and Too Much Junk Food	Stan and Jan Berenstain	Fiction • Narrative
	I Will Never Not Ever Eat a Tomato	Lauren Child	Fiction • Narrative

14	Madeline	Ludwig Bemelmans	Fiction • Realistic Narrative
	The Berenstain Bears Go to the Doctor	Stan and Jan Berenstain	Fiction • Narrative
15	Officer Buckle and Gloria	Peggy Rathmann	Fiction • Narrative
	Make Way for Ducklings	Robert McCloskey	Fiction • Narrative
16	Honk!	Pamela Duncan Edwards	Fiction • Narrative
	Lili Backstage	Rachel Isadora	Fiction • Narrative
17	Moses Goes to a Concert	Issac Millman	Fiction • Narrative
	The Remarkable Farkle McBride	John Lithgow	Fiction • Rhyming Narrative
18	Miss Tizzy	Libba Moore Gray	Fiction • Narrative
	Amazing Grace	Mary Hoffman	Fiction • Narrative
19	Honey: A Gift From Nature	Yumiko Fujiwara	Fiction • Narrative With Factual Content
	Winnie-the-Pooh and Some Bees	adapted by Stephen Krensky	Fiction • Narrative
	Berlioz the Bear	Jan Brett	Fiction • Narrative
20	The Carrot Seed	Ruth Kraus	Fiction • Narrative
	Flower Garden	Mary Hoffman	Fiction • Narrative
21	Just You and Me	Sam McBratney	Fiction • Narrative
	Over in the Meadow	Jack Ezra Keats, illustrator	Fiction • Rhyming Narrative
22	Lobster's Secret	Kathleen M. Hollenbeck	Fiction • Narrative With Factual Content
	Commotion in the Ocean	Giles Andreae	Fiction • Rhyming Narrative With Factual Content
23	Gentle Giant Octopus	Karen Wallace	Nonfiction • Narrative
	Down in the Sea: The Octopus	Patricia Kite	Nonfiction • Expository
24	Mama, Do You Love Me?	Barbara M. Joosse	Fiction • Narrative
	Stella, Star of the Sea	Mary Louise Gay	Fiction • Narrative
25	The Relatives Came	Cynthia Rylant	Fiction • Realistic Narrative
	Yoko's Paper Cranes	Rosemary Wells	Fiction • Narrative
26	Dr. Seuss's ABC	Dr. Seuss	Fiction • Rhyming Narrative
	A My Name Is . . .	Alice Lyne	Alphabet Book

Red = Books included in the *Read Well K* Children's Literature Set

Whole Class Word Lists

Reading and Spelling Words

All words listed are read by students. Words in red are also spelled by students. Bold indicates the word's first appearance.

By Unit

Unit	Sound Sequence	Sound Spell	Pattern Words	Irregular (Tricky) Words
1	Aa			
2	Ee			
3	Hh	Aa, ee		I
4	Kk			I
5	Mm	Mm		I
6	Rr	Hh	**I'm**	I
7	Ss	Ss	I'm, **me**	I
8	ee, Ww		**am**, I'm, me, **Sam**, see	I
9	Zz	Ww	am, **he**, I'm, me, Sam, see, **See**, **we**	I
R			am, I'm, me, Sam, see, See, we	I
10	Cc	Rr	am, he, I'm, me, Sam, see, we	I
11	Dd	Dd	am, **dad**, **ham**, he, I'm, me, Sam, see, See, we, **We**	I, **the**, **The**
12	Ii	Ii	am, dad, **Dad**, **had**, he, I'm, **mad**, **sad**, see, we	I, the
13	Jj	Cc	am, Dad, **did**, had, I'm, mad, me, sad, Sam, see, See, we	I, the
14	Nn		**Am**, am, did, had, he, I'm, mad, me, Sam, see, See, we	I, **is**, the
15	Pp	Nn	**an**, **and**, **can**, did, **had**, me, see, See, we	I, is
16	Tt	Pp	am, an, and, can, **Can**, had, he, I'm, **in**, mad, me, Sam, see, See	I, is, the
17	Vv	Tt	an, and, **at**, can, **cat**, did, had, he, in, mad, **man**, sad, **sat**, see, **sit**, we	I, is, the

Unit	Sound Sequence	Sound Spell	Pattern Words	Irregular (Tricky) Words
18	Yy		and, at, can, cat, dad, did, had, he, **it**, mad, Sam, sat, see, See, sit, we, We, **This**	**his**, I, is, **Is**, the
E	Ee (short)	E (short)	am, an, and, at, can, dad, did, **Ed**, had, **Had**, He, in, it, mad, me, sad, sat, see, See, we	**a**, the
19	Bb	Vv	am, an, at, **bad**, **bat**, cat, had, **hat**, in, mad, man, me, sat, see, See, van, we	a, I, the, The
20	Ff		and, at, bad, bat, **big**, Ed, had, in, it, he, me, **need**, sad, sat, see, See, **seed**, we, We	a, I, the
21	Gg	Ff	am, an, and, at, bad, bat, cat, Ed, **fat**, **fed**, **Fed**, he, in, me, need, sad, sat, see, See, seed	a, I, **said**, the
22	Ll	Gg	at, **bat**, **big**, cat, did, in, it, me, **pen**, **pig**, sat, see, See, we, We	a, I, is, the, The, was
23	Oo	Oo	and, at, bad, bat, **be**, **bee**, **dig**, dog, Ed, had, he, in, it, **jig**, **log**, need, not, sad, sat, see, seed, ten, van, we	a, have, **Have**, I, is, said, the, The, was
24	Qq	Ll	and, bad, bat, be, bee, big, dad, did, dog, Ed, had, he, log, pet, see, See, we, **We**	a, have, Have, I, is, said, the, The, was
25	Uu	Uu	an, at, bag, bat, **bed**, big, **but**, cat, **cut**, dad, did, dog, in, it, jig, **nut**, **on**, **pan**, **pig**, **run**, sat, see	a, have, I, is, the, The, was
26	Xx		an, bag, be, bee, big, but, can, **cut**, dad, did, dog, Ed, in, on, **red**, sad, see, See, **This**, van, we, We	a, have, I, is, said, the, The
R			and, bed, big, **dig**, dog, **dug**, fat, **hen**, in, me, **men**, **met**, **Met**, **nest**, **net**, pig, red, run, see, See, ten, **up**, we, We, **wet**, **win**	a, I, is, the
VR			am, **ant**, bag, bat, bee, **beet**, **beg**, **bet**, big, **bug**, but, can, cat, **cub**, cut, dad, did, dog, hat, hen, in, it, **jet**, log, mad, **man**, men, met, nest, net, on, **pen**, pig, red, **rug**, run, sad, sat, see, See, **set**, sit, ten, **tub**, **us**, We, wet	a, I, is, the, The

Cumulative (all units)

Pattern Words	Irregular (Tricky) Words
am, Am, an, and, ant, at, bad, bag, bat, be, bed, bee, beet, beg, bet, big, bug, but, can, Can, cat, cub, cut, dad, Dad, did, dig, dog, dug, Ed, fat, fed, Fed, had, Had, ham, hat, he, He, hen, I'm, in, it, jet, jig, log, mad, man, me, men, met, Met, need, nest, net, not, nut, on, pan, pen, pet, pig, red, rug, run, sad, Sam, sat, see, See, seed, set, sit, ten, This, tub, up, us, van, we, We, wet, win	a, have, **Have**, his, I, is, **Is**, said, the, The, was

Oral Vocabulary

Unit	New in Each Unit
1	ant, custodian, librarian, principal, secretary
2	animal, binoculars, gym, library, office, playground
3	field trip, glider, journal, letter
4	rhyming words
5	cap, copy, peddler
6	farm, friend, teamwork
7	abdomen, arachnid, author, dew, glistening, interrupt, spider, spiderweb, spinneret
8	burrow, earthworm/worm, vibration
9	exhausted, unique, zoo
Rev	*(Students review previous vocabulary in this unit.)*
10	forlorn, incessant, illustrator
11	adventure, blind, officer, protect, rescue, taxi, uniform
12	anatomy, antennae, fact, head, insect, thorax
13	blues, distraught, habit, healthy food, junk food, talent
14	accident, ambulance, distracted, doctor's bag, hospital, paramedic, scar, stethoscope
15	emergency, whine
16	audience, ballet, determined, fierce, performance, rehearsal, swan
17	American Sign Language, concert, deaf, orchestra, theater
18	disappeared, mystery, peculiar, scarf
E	fiction
19	bee, communicate, hero, hive, nectar
20	energy, garden, selfish, share, soil
21	alarmed, gander, gosling
22	claws, kindness, molt, stunned
23	octopus, perplexed
24	angry, concerned, island, occasion, quilt, relative
25	perfect, unusual
26	clue, detective
Rev	setting
V Rev	sturdy

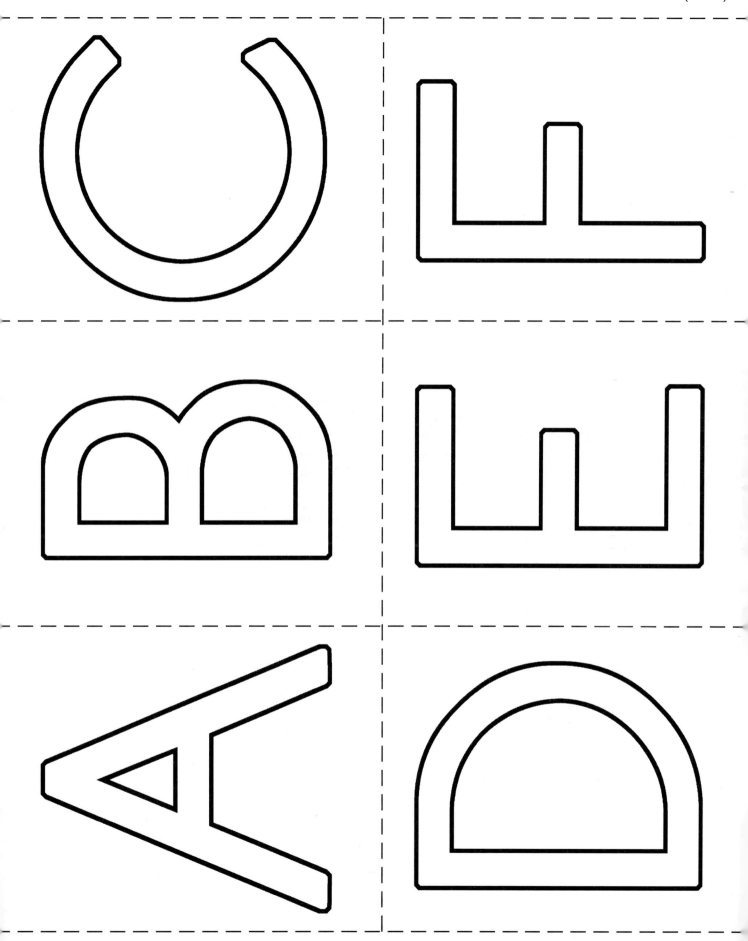

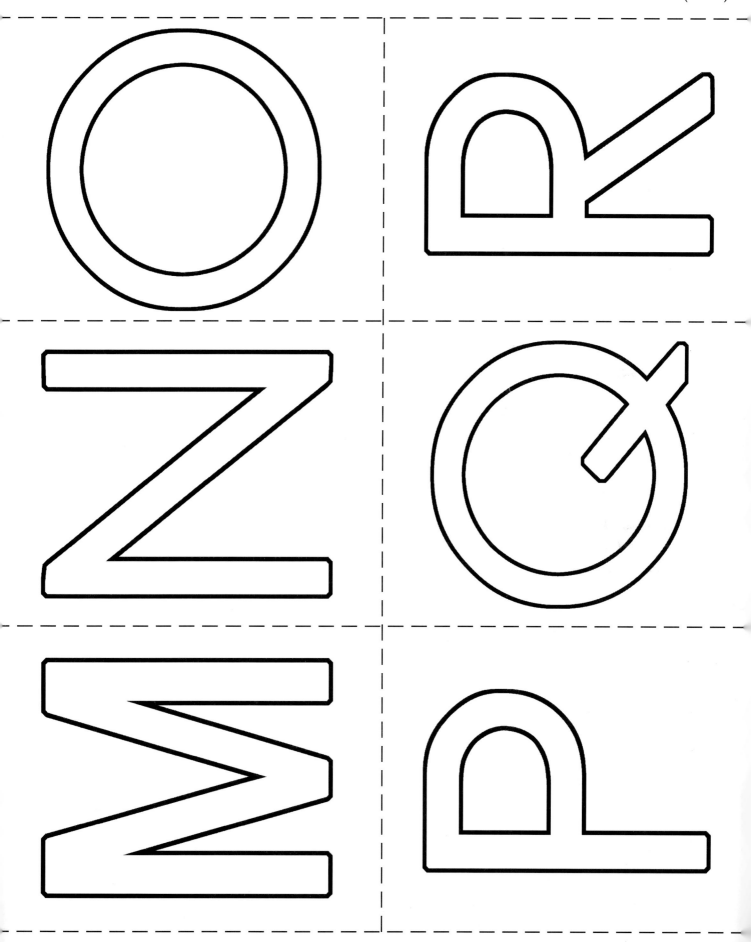

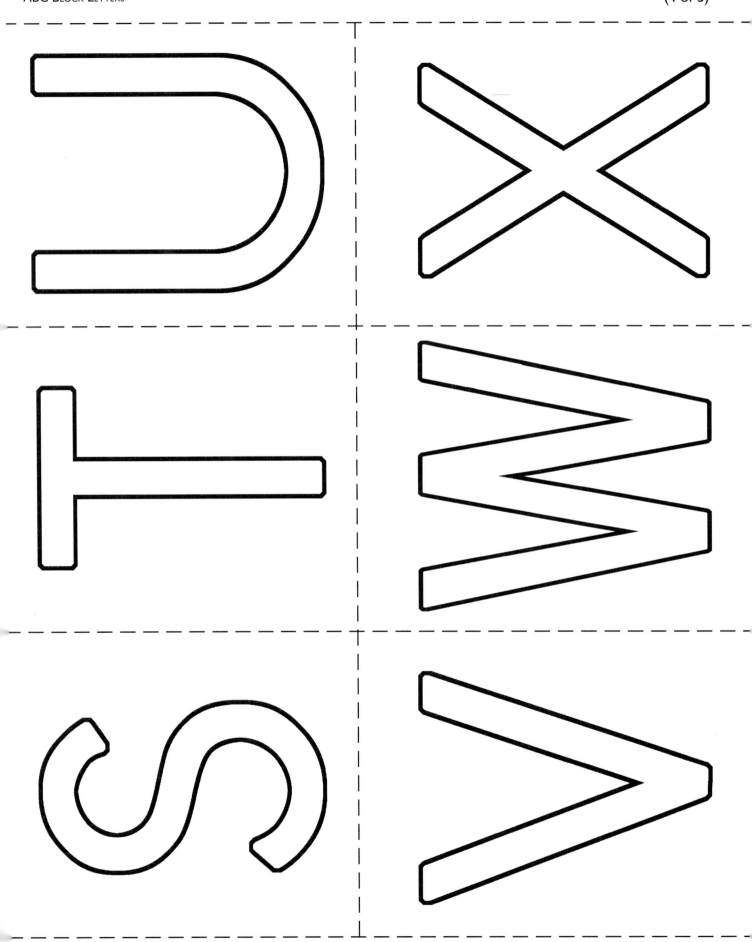

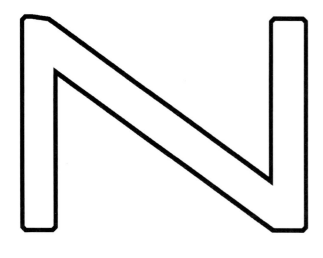

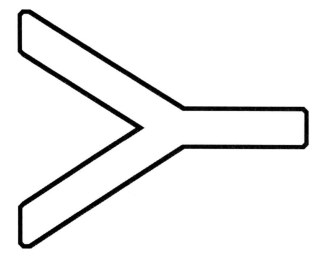

My Journal

| A | B | C | D | E | F | G |

Z · Y · X · W · V · U (left column)

H · I · J · K · L · M (right column)

T · S · R · Q · P · O · N (bottom row)

I'm

Read Well K • Blackline Master

I'm

I'm

Read Well K • Blackline Master

I'm _____

Adams, M. J. (1990). *Beginning to read: Thinking and learning about print*. Cambridge, MA: MIT Press.

Anderson, L. W., Krathwohl, D. R., Airasian, P. W., Cruikshank, K. A., Mayer, R. E., Pintrich, P. R., et al. (2000). *A Taxonomy for Learning, Teaching, and Assessing: A Revision of Bloom's Taxonomy of Educational Objectives*. New York, NY: Longman.

Anderson, R. C., Hiebert, E., Scott, J., & Wilkinson, I. (1985). *Becoming a nation of readers: The report of the commission on reading*. Washington, DC: The National Institute of Education.

Archer, A. (2001, January 9). *New Mexico's mission to read*. Speech presented for the Statewide Professional Development for Reading, Albuquerque, NM.

Armbruster, B. B., Lehr, F., & Osborn, J. (2001). *Put reading first: The research building blocks for teaching children to read*. Washington, DC: National Institute for Literacy.

Baker, S. K., Simmons, D. C., & Kame'enui, E. J. (1998). Vocabulary acquisition: Research bases. In D. Carnine & E. Kame'enui (Eds.), *What reading research tells us about children with diverse learning needs: Bases and basics* (pp. 183–217). Mahwah, NJ: Lawrence Erlbaum Associates.

Ball, E., & Blachman, B. A. (1991). Does phoneme awareness training in kindergarten make a difference in early word recognition and developmental spelling? *Reading Research Quarterly, 26*(1), 49–66.

Baumann, J. F., & Bergeron, B. (1993). Story map instruction using children's literature: Effects on first graders' comprehension of narrative elements. *Journal of Reading Behavior, 25*(4), 407–437.

Baumann, J. F., & Kame'enui, E. J. (1991). Research on vocabulary instruction: Ode to Voltaire. In J. Flood, J. Jensen, D. Lapp, & J. R. Squire (Eds.), *Handbook of research on teaching the English language arts* (pp. 604–632). New York: Macmillan.

Beck, I. L., & McKeown, M. G. (1981). Developing questions that promote comprehension: The story map. *Language Arts, 58*(8), 913–918.

Beck, I. L., & McKeown, M. G. (2001). Text talk: Capturing the benefits of read-aloud experiences for young children. *The Reading Teacher, 55*(1), 10–20.

Beck, I. L., McKeown, M. G., & Kucan, L. (2002). *Bringing Words to Life: Robust Vocabulary Instruction*. New York, NY: Guilford Press.

Beck, I. L., McKeown, M. G., & Kucan, L. (2003, Spring). Taking delight in words: Using oral language to build young children's vocabularies. *American Educator, 27*(1), 36–46.

Beck, I. L., Omanson, R. C., & McKeown, M. G. (1982). An instructional redesign of reading lessons: Effects on comprehension. *Reading Research Quarterly, 17*(4), 462–481.

Biemiller, A. (1999). *Language and reading success: From reading research to practice* (Vol. 5). Cambridge, MA: Brookline Books.

Biemiller, A. (2000) Vocabulary: The missing link between phonics and comprehension. *Perspectives, 26*(4), 26–30.

Biemiller, A. (Spring, 2003). Oral comprehension sets the ceiling on reading comprehension. *American Federation of Teachers, 23*.

Byrne, B., & Fielding-Barnsley, R. (1991). Evaluation of a program to teach phonemic awareness to young children. *Journal of Educational Psychology, 83*(4), 451–455.

Carnine, D., Silbert, J., & Kameenui, E. (1990). *Direct instruction reading*. Columbus, OH: Merrill Publishing Company.

Carroll, J.B., Davies, P., & Richman, B. (1971). *The American heritage word frequency book*. Boston: Houghton Mifflin.

Chall, J. S., & Jacobs, V. A. (2003, Spring). Poor children's fourth-grade slump. *American Educator, 27*(1), 14, 44.

Selected References (*continued*)

Chall, J. S., Jacobs, V. A., & Baldwin, L. E. (1990). *The reading crisis: Why poor children fall behind.* Cambridge, MA: Harvard University Press.

Denton, C. A., Anthony, J. L., Parker, R., & Hasbrouck, J. E. (2004). Effects of two tutoring programs on the English reading development of Spanish-English bilingual students. *The Elementary School Journal, 104*(4), 289–305.

Dowhower, S. L. (1991). Speaking of prosody: Fluency's unattended bedfellow. *Theory Into Practice, 30,* 165–175.

Ehri, L. C., Nunes, S. R., Willows, D. M., Schuster, B. V., Yaghoub-Zadeh, Z., & Shanahan, T. (2001). Phonemic awareness instruction helps children learn to read: Evidence from the national reading panel's meta-analysis. *Reading Research Quarterly, 36*(3), 250–287.

Foorman, B. R., & Torgesen, J. (2001). Critical elements of classroom and small-group instruction promote reading success in all children. *Learning Disabilities: Research & Practice, 16*(4), 203–212.

Foorman, B. R., Francis, D. J., Fletcher, J. M., Mehta, P., & Schatschneider, C. (1998). The role of instruction in learning to read: Preventing reading failure in at-risk children. *Journal of Educational Psychology, 90*(1), 37–55.

Fry, E. B., Kress, J. E., & Fountoukidis, D. L. (2000). *The reading teacher's book of lists.* San Francisco: Jossey-Bass.

Fuchs, D., Fuchs, L. S., Thompson, A., Al Otaiba, S., Yen, L., Yang, N. J., Braun, M., & O'Connor, R. (2001). Is reading important in reading-readiness programs? A randomized field trial with teachers as program implementers. *Journal of Educational Psychology, 93*(2), 251–267.

Hansen, R. A., & Farrell, D. (1995). The long-term effects on high school seniors of learning to read in kindergarten. *Reading Research Quarterly, 30,* 908–933.

Hart, B., & Risley, T. (1995). *Meaningful differences in the everyday experience of young American children.* Baltimore, MA: Paul H. Brookes.

Hasbrouck, J., & Tindal, G. (2005). *Oral reading fluency: 90 years of measurement* (Tech. Rep. No. 33). Eugene, OR: University of Oregon, College of Education, Behavioral Research and Teaching.

Hirsch, E. D. (2003, Spring). Reading comprehension requires knowledge—of words and the world. *American Educator, 27,* 10–48.

International Reading Association and National Association for the Education of Young Children (1998). Learning to read and write: Developmentally appropriate practices for young children. *The Reading Teacher, 52,* 193–216.

Juel, C. (1988). Learning to read and write: A longitudinal study of 54 children from first through fourth grades. *Journal of Educational Psychology, 80*(4), 437–447.

Learning First Alliance. (1998). *Every child reading: An action plan.* Washington, DC: Author.

National Reading Panel. (2000). *Report of the national reading panel.* Washington, DC: National Institute of Child Health and Human Development.

Ogle, D. (1986). K-W-L: A teaching model that develops active reading of expository text. *The Reading Teacher, 39,* 564–570.

Samuels, S. J., & Flor, R. F. (1997). The importance of automaticity for developing expertise in reading. *Reading and Writing Quarterly, 13,* 107–121.

Snow, C. E., Burns, M. S., & Griffin, P. (Eds.). (1998). *Preventing reading difficulties in young children.* Washington, DC: National Academy Press.

Sprick, R., Garrison, M., & Howard, L. (1998). *CHAMPs: A proactive and positive approach to classroom management.* Longmont, CO: Sopris West.

Stahl, S. A. (2003). How words are learned incrementally over multiple exposures. *American Educator, 27*(1), 18–19, 44.

Stahl, S., Osborn, J., & Lehr, F. (1990). *Beginning to read: Thinking and learning about print. A Summary.* Urbana-Champaign, IL: University of Illinois, Center for the Study of Reading.

Torgesen, J. K. (2004). Avoiding the devastating downward spiral: The evidence that early intervention prevents reading failure. *American Educator, 28*(3), 6–19.

Vaughn, S., & Linan-Thompson, S. (2004). *Research-based methods of reading instruction, grades K–3.* Alexandria, VA: Association for Supervision and Curriculum Development.

What Works Clearinghouse; Institute of Education Sciences; U.S. Department of Education. (2006). WWC Intervention Report: Read Well. Retrieved September 21, 2006 from http://www.whatworks.ed.gov/PDF/Intervention/WWC Read Well 092106.pdf.

Yopp, H. K. (1992). Developing phonemic awareness in young children. *The Reading Teacher, 45*(9), 696–703.